filled

filled

**60 Devotions for the
Foster Parent's Heart**

jamie c. finn

BakerBooks

a division of Baker Publishing Group
BakerBooks.com

Library of Congress Cataloging-in-Publication Data
Names: Finn, Jamie C., 1984– author.
Title: Filled : 60 devotions for the foster parent's heart / Jamie C. Finn.
Description: Grand Rapids, Michigan : Baker Books, a division of Baker Publishing Group, [2024]
   | Includes bibliographical references.
Identifiers: LCCN 2023043290 | ISBN 9781540904034 (cloth) | ISBN 9781493445806 (ebook)
Subjects: LCSH: Foster parents—Religious life. | Parenting—Religious aspects—Christianity. |
   Devotional literature.
Classification: LCC BV4529.16 .F55 2024 | DDC 248.8/45—dc23/eng/20240226
LC record available at https://lccn.loc.gov/2023043290

24   25   26   27   28   29   30   7   6   5   4   3   2   1

For Liv, Wes, Bella, Em, and Jax.
I have so many hopes for you,
but none greater than the hope
that you come to know and treasure
the surpassing worth of Jesus above all else.
I love you so much. He loves you more.

———

"I pray that you . . . grasp how wide and long and
high and deep is the love of Christ, and . . . know
this love that surpasses knowledge—that you
may be filled to the measure of all the fullness
of God." (Eph. 3:17–19)

a note from jamie

It's 7:07 a.m.

You have searched me, Lord, and You know me. You know when I sit and when I rise; You perceive my thoughts from afar.

My toddler runs to the couch, hand reaching for my inspection. "Uh-oh, Mommy, uh-oh. Isss messy. Isss yucky. Hand yucky."

I inspect the brown smear on his hand. "What is it? Jax. What is this? Is it poop or chocolate? *Is this poop or chocolate?*" He laughs. I employ the safest method of determining the "poop or chocolate" dilemma we regularly find ourselves in and smell his hand. It doesn't smell much of anything, so I go for the second, riskier but surer method: taste. "It's chocolate," I proclaim with relief.

His smile breaks into a full belly giggle. "Chocolate!" he concurs.

You hem me in behind and before, and You lay Your hand upon me. Such knowledge is too wonderful for me, too lofty for me to attain.

My teenager is accusing someone of unplugging her AirPods. Because she knows she plugged them in and AirPods don't just unplug themselves and now they are going to die and she won't be able to listen to music when she's walking in the halls at school, and do you know how obnoxious people are in the hallways at school and how is she even supposed to get through the day, and are you even listening to me, Mom? Mom?

I praise You because I am fearfully and wonderfully made; Your works are wonderful, I know that full well.

My middles add to the chorus.

"Can I have more cereal?"

"She's crossing her legs toward me, and she knows I hate when she crosses her legs toward me."

"Are those my pants you're wearing?"

"He farted near me—on purpose."

"Mom said we could only watch a show if we could agree on one, and I hate this show."

"Shoot, I forgot I have a test today."

Search me, God, and know my heart; test me and know my anxious thoughts. See if there is any offensive way in me, and lead me in the way everlasting.

I've had to redefine "quiet times." Calling something by a name that it decidedly isn't is not only misleading, it is certain to brew disappointment. It might be more accurately branded "loud time" in my home, but that doesn't quite capture the intention of the practice.

Spending time in God's Word in real life doesn't usually look like it does on Instagram. You know the carefully curated square I'm calling out. Two hands wrapped around a steaming mug of a perfectly crafted latte, complete with one of those barista-caliber leafy-pattern things in the foam. A white (White? Are you kidding me?) cable-knit blanket draped across a wicker chair with a clear view of the #NoFilter burnt-orange sun rising over trees, leaves suspended in the air between swaying branches, and dew-covered grass.

My real-life, not-at-all-quiet times include a worn-out Bible with notes along the margins, a couple of dog-eared books strewn across the couch, a chipped mug containing my fourth cup of coffee, and—as previously discussed—noisy kids and some form of chocolate/poop.

Don't get me wrong, approaching the God of the universe, consuming the words of the sacred Book He supernaturally penned is a wonderfully, fearfully sacred practice. It is truly holy ground. But the believers of the Bible needed bare feet, burning coals, and bleeding bulls to approach, and—covered in the blood of Jesus and gifted words inspired by the Holy Spirit—I need simply to crack open a book. My daily Bible reading is, at the very least, a spiritual discipline—a chore done in faith and obedience, even when I don't "feel" the fruit of it—and at its best, my very source for this life of foster parenting.

I need God's Word each day because, well, being a foster parent is hard. I offer other flowery elaborations on that word—*hard*—throughout this book, but mostly, it's just hard. Like *hard* hard. I've stepped into the broken stories of broken people, and I find my heart cracked wide open by it all. From the daily mundane duties of paperwork and visits to the existential struggles of injustice and loss, I am weighed down by the heavy burdens of foster care. And I am in desperate, daily need of something to lift me from under its load.

His Word is what I need most—more than any training or strategy, more than help or rest or any other legitimate need that I legitimately have. I need the supernatural encouragement and teaching and guidance that only His Holy Word and Spirit can provide. God communicates with clarity and comfort and command for all of life through Scripture. Do you believe that He has something to say, specifically, to you as a foster parent? Something that can change the way you walk, think, and feel? I do, and I have experienced it for the ten years of my foster parenting journey. You won't find the words *foster care* in the Bible, but that doesn't mean it doesn't speak directly to us.

   I am a firstborn. Not just a firstborn, but a firstborn *daughter*. So read between the lines and hear what I'm trying to tell you: I'm bossy. But try not to take it that way. You see, I've labored over this book. I have prayed and studied, poured out my story and failures and intimate thoughts in its pages, and I want you to hear my heart for you as you read it. So here are some—*ahem*—suggestions for going through this book.

Read It Slowly

I am a fast eater. I'm just so eager to try all the things that I speed through a meal and then (while nursing my aching belly) sit and watch my dinner mates slowly enjoy their food. But did you know that food actually tastes better when you eat it slowly? Yeah, it has something to do with breathing, which apparently I skip in my voracious gobbling.

   You could probably fly through the pages of this book in a couple hours' time, but I beg you not to. This isn't a book of content to consume; it's a collection of readings to bring you small morsels of encouragement each day. If this book were food, it wouldn't be a bowl of ice cream, meant to be quickly devoured and fill you up; it would be a box of chocolates, meant to be slowly savored and tasted, one by one. So breathe, go slowly, and enjoy.

Read the Scripture

Let me tell you how—left to my own devices—I would read this devotional: Skim over the Scripture. *Got it. Recognize this one, know it already. Let me get to the good stuff now.* As if, somehow, Jamie Finn could write something worth your attention over and above the God of the universe. Read the verse. Meditate on it. If it's lengthy, maybe underline the key words. But please don't pass it over.

Read with Prayer

Refuse to close the binding of this book without spending one minute—sixty seconds—praying that God would help you to understand, believe, and apply what you've read. We need more than my inadequate writing abilities and limited understanding of Scripture or your ability to understand, focus, and apply to get us through this together. Pray that the Holy Spirit would bring encouragement, conviction, and action from your time of reading that only He can bring.

Read It as *Part* of Your Devotional Time

I cannot emphasize this enough: This book is not meant to replace your daily Bible reading; it is meant to enhance it. You need God's words so much more than you need mine.

I've often heard encouragements to busy moms about their lack of Bible reading that equate to something like "Give yourself grace, God knows you're busy and tired, He'll take care of you." Great points on all fronts—*all* is grace, God knows your burdens better than *any*, and He *will* take care of you. But I want to challenge you to consider that maybe even more than "too

busy" or "too tired," you are "too desperate." You are—as I am—
too desperate, this life is *too* hard, and there is *too* much at stake
for the both of us to be walking around relying on our wisdom
and strength. We are desperately in need of what God offers us
in His Word.

I want to encourage you to carve out enough time—
preferably in the morning but at least some regular time each
day—to read a portion of God's Word and pray. If you have
a plan, stick with that. If not, I've recommended a passage of
Scripture that complements each daily reading. Think for a moment: How would sixty days of consistent Bible reading change
your heart, your thoughts, your foster parenting? A commitment
like this takes sacrifice, certainly, but more than that, it takes
faith. Do you believe that you need God's Word more than you
need anything else on this earth? How should this belief change
what time you wake up, your exercise routine, how much TV or
social media you consume?

Do not allow this devotional to replace a time of devotion
to God—reading His Word, praying, and worshiping Him. My
prayer is that this book serves as a gateway into exploring, for
yourself, the truths of God's Word that apply to your life and
foster parenting. May this book, more than anything, whet your
appetite for the treasure of Scripture.

◆▼◆

For ten years, I have struggled and stumbled through this
journey of foster parenting. I've experienced the greatest joys
and sorrows of my life. I've known the deepest depths of fear
and the highest heights of happiness. I have wrestled through
devastating realities and unanswerable questions. I have failed
and fallen time and time again.

And through all of it, His Word has carried me. I have found the glorious truths of God's sovereign grace to be the answer to nearly every question. I have experienced the salve of His comforting promises for my anxieties, fears, and cravings for control. I have heard His direction and guidance through the bewildering and uncertain. I have been convicted and corrected for the ways I've walked. Most of all, I have come to know and experience the love of Jesus in a way that's filled me, sustained me, transformed me.

So, friend, I invite you to journey through God's Word with me. I pray that together, we "grasp how wide and long and high and deep is the love of Christ, and . . . know this love that surpasses knowledge—that [we] may be filled to the measure of all the fullness of God" (Eph. 3:18–19).

The law of the LORD is perfect,
    refreshing the soul.
The statutes of the LORD are trustworthy,
    making wise the simple.
The precepts of the LORD are right,
    giving joy to the heart.
The commands of the LORD are radiant,
    giving light to the eyes.
The fear of the LORD is pure,
    enduring forever.
The decrees of the LORD are firm,
    and all of them are righteous.

They are more precious than gold,
    than much pure gold;
they are sweeter than honey,
    than honey from the honeycomb.
By them your servant is warned;
    in keeping them there is great reward.
But who can discern their own errors?
    Forgive my hidden faults.
Keep your servant also from willful sins;
    may they not rule over me.
Then I will be blameless,
    innocent of great transgression.

May these words of my mouth
    and this meditation of my heart
    be pleasing in your sight.

1

> Your word is a lamp to my feet
> and a light to my path.
>
> Psalm 119:105 ESV

My dad got mad and pushed me down the stairs, and I couldn't walk for a while—it was no big deal."

"The judge didn't even look up from the papers while I told him what they had done to me."

"I love her so much, but I just can't stop using, no matter how hard I try. I promise I really do love her."

"In the middle of the night, I see the bad man, and I remember what he did to me."

Dark things brought into the light, confessed to me with side glances of shame by hurting children and parents.

There is a darkness to foster care, a darkness I didn't realize I would be surrounded by, walking through, inviting into my home when I became a foster parent. Sometimes it feels as though I am walking through the very valley of the shadow of death, a place where the bright and good that family and justice and wholeness should be have become dim and dark and distorted.

I need a light and a lamp, something supernatural to illuminate the way.

Enter the light-bearing Word. The miracle of the gospel is that God sent the Word—His only Son—to make Himself known to His created beings. The miracle of Scripture is that He gave His written Word to continue to make Himself known to His created beings.

The Word—God's written Word, recorded in Scripture—is not just a place where we come to know *about* God. It is the place where we actually come to know God Himself. The words that make up the Word of God are not simply letters and phonemes. They are "living and active" (Heb. 4:12 ESV), "breathed out by God and profitable" (2 Tim. 3:16 ESV)—this isn't poetry; this is fact. Scripture is alive and accomplishing, brought to life by the mouth of God Himself. His Word has the supernatural power to "impart understanding" (Ps. 119:130 ESV) and "sanctify [us] in the truth" (John 17:17 ESV). It is not a "human word, but . . . the word of God, which is indeed at work in you" (1 Thess. 2:13). As my feet step into dark spaces, the Word serves as a lamp. As I walk along a dim path, the Word brings light. Because "the unfolding of [His] words gives light" (Ps. 119:130).

This is not only because wisdom and direction are found in His Word; it is because *He*—the Word, Jesus Himself—is found in His Word. "The Word [is] God" (John 1:1), and He is "the true light that gives light to everyone" (v. 9). When Jesus stepped into darkness and claimed, "I am the light of the world," He promised, "whoever follows me will not walk in darkness, but will have the light of life" (8:12 ESV). It is not just principles and precepts that we need; it is Jesus. Reading His words and His miracles in the Gospels, learning the truths of His death and resurrection in the epistles, seeing His ultimate glory in Revelation—these reveal the Savior to us and invite us into worship of Him and relationship with Him. The glory of the Word (Scripture) is that it is there that we see glories of the Word (Jesus).

Foster care is a dark place full of evil and pain and injustice. But "the light shines in the darkness, and the darkness has not overcome it" (1:5). He, the Light of the World, is with you. And not just with you and watching. With you and leading. With you and providing. With you and lighting the way.

FURTHER READING

John 1; Psalm 19

2

For we are his workmanship, created in
Christ Jesus for good works, which God
prepared beforehand, that we should walk
in them.

Ephesians 2:10 ESV

"F oster mom." It's a title so unique and so defining that it's at risk of becoming the thing by which I most identify myself. Much of my time and focus are spent on visits and behaviors and workers and biological parents. Even between placements, there's still the web of family connections, the stinging losses, the stress of waiting for calls, or the anguish of saying no to them.

Ask me to define myself in two words, and I'd be tempted to say "foster mom." But I'd be wrong. The best definition takes only one word: *daughter*.

As a child of God, nothing that I do is the most important thing about me. And foster parenting is something that I do. It is not who I am. When I put my actions before my identity, I am building on a changeable, faulty foundation. Right now, I am wife to Alan and mom to Liv, Wes, Bella, Em, Jax, and Dillon. And not to be morbid, but even this most important part of what I do with my life could be taken from me in an instant.

The only completely constant, unchangeable and unchanging, irremovable and unflinching part of me? That I am His. And this is what is most reliable about me. Why? Because it is based on *Him* and not on me. He is constant. His grace is unchangeable and His mercy is unchanging. His adoption of me is irremovable and His love for me is unflinching.

Who I am is, simply put, based on who He is rather than who I am.

Ephesians 2:10 reminds us that we were *created* to do good works. But you simply cannot consider the meaning of Ephesians 2:10 without the rich verses that precede and define and inform it:

> **And you were dead in the trespasses and sins** in which you once walked, following the course of this world, following the prince of the power of the air, the spirit that is now at work in the sons of disobedience—among whom we all once lived in the passions of our flesh, carrying out the desires of the body and the mind, and were by nature children of wrath, like the rest of mankind. **But God, being rich in mercy, because of the great love with which he loved us,** even when we were dead in our trespasses, **made us alive together with Christ**—by grace you have been saved—and raised us up with him and seated us with him in the heavenly places in Christ Jesus, **so that in the coming ages he might show the immeasurable riches of his grace** in kindness toward us in Christ Jesus. **For by grace you have been saved through faith. And this is not your own doing; it is the gift of God, not a result of works,** so that no one may boast. (vv. 1–9 ESV, emphasis mine)

We were created and commissioned by God to do things for Him and for others that are so eternal, they were prepared before we were even born. This is big news.

But preceding this commission is a reminder of our identity.

We were dead (v. 1).

We were loved, with great love (v. 4).

We were made alive and one with Christ (v. 5).

We were saved to exalt the riches of His grace (v. 7).

We had nothing to do with our salvation. It is a gift of grace from God (vv. 8–9).

The full gospel message of this passage is absolutely crucial to the "good works" battle cry we pull from it. We must guard against putting the proverbial foster-care-mission cart before the saved-by-grace-alone horse.

Foster care is a mission—a grand and glorious, eternal mission. Spending up your days loving and serving the people involved in it is good, good work. And good works are important—we were created to do them! But good works must proceed from what precedes them. Namely, our identity in Him. Our works are not what define us, not what identify us, and they never save us. The saving work is His, and it's only ever "the gift of God, not a result of works" (vv. 8–9 ESV).

You are called to do for Him, but first and foremost, you are His.

FURTHER READING

2 Corinthians 5

3

He has shown you, O mortal, what is good.
> And what does the LORD require of you?
To act justly and to love mercy
> and to walk humbly with your God.

Micah 6:8

We walk through the doors of the clinic, hand in hand. The sign bears a cutesy name that doesn't at all reflect the nature of what happens inside its walls. We're greeted by a grandma-looking greeter whose sole purpose is to play with my child in the playroom as I talk to the doctor. I sit in the designated seat, shivering from the cold examination room as well as the anxiety surging through my body. I tell her what I know—that this child came home from a visit with this on their body, that I called the worker immediately. The child enters the room with grandma-greeter, shrinks into my lap, and nods as I say, "We need to show the doctor." The doctor undresses the child and reveals a six-inch black bruise. The doctor measures and photographs and documents. I sit back and seethe.

People should be punished for hurting children. No one should get away with the crimes that the kids in my home have had to endure at the hands of those who should've protected them. Our hearts mirror our God's heart when we love justice. "For I, the LORD, love justice," He says in Isaiah 61:8. "All his ways are justice," Deuteronomy 32:4 (ESV) proclaims. He is a just God, and as His image bearers, we carry within us the ache for things to be made right, the drive for justice to win.

But God is never only one of His characteristics; He is always all of them. Along with His justice stands His mercy. "God, who is rich in mercy" (Eph. 2:4), is "merciful and gracious, slow to anger, and abounding in steadfast love and faithfulness" (Exod. 34:6 ESV). Our God is a merciful God. And as His image bearers, we carry within us an innate mercy that is driven to step into broken places with compassion.

God's justice is like the black-velvet cloth that magnifies the glistening diamond of His mercy. His justice couldn't leave our damnable sin unpunished, so in a great act of mercy, "God presented Christ" (Rom. 3:25) to take our punishment "so as to be just and the one who justifies" (v. 26). We are now "justified freely by his grace" (v. 24). At the cross of Christ, justice was satisfied, and mercy was applied. As recipients of this great gospel exchange, we should be the first ones to celebrate mercy as we hold justice.

Justice and mercy are brought to perfection in relationship to each other, and we are called to maintain justice, mercy, and humility together in unity. Zechariah 7:9 echoes their sacred pairing again with the call to "administer true justice" and "show mercy and compassion."

We like to talk about justice in situations like child abuse. It feels right to cry out for what's right when someone else has done the wrong. But mercy? Yeah, that's kept for people a little more deserving, people more like me. Oh, friend, Jesus came for "them" and for me, just the same. He came for middle-class moms who do nice things, and He came for child abusers. Jesus loves people like me, and Jesus loves people like "them."

I need the punishment I deserve to be removed just as desperately as anyone else does. And as someone whose sin demanded the justice of God and received the mercy, I should be the first to hold justice and extend mercy.

So, what does the Lord require of us as foster parents? As we bring our beloved children to child abuse examinations and as we fail and fall ourselves? "To act justly and to love mercy and to walk humbly."

FURTHER READING

Romans 3

4

Bear with each other and forgive one another if any of you has a grievance against someone. Forgive as the Lord forgave you.

Colossians 3:13

O h, loving the kids is the easy part," a foster-mom friend proclaims to a group of moms nodding in agreement. "It's everyone else who makes foster care hard. But loving the kids? That's easy."

I nod along, like someone who isn't on the inside of the inside joke but is too embarrassed to admit it. *Yeah, loving the kids is so easy. EASY. Not hard at all, just easy peasy, lemon squeezy.*

Last night I left my child alone in their room because I couldn't protect myself from their violent blows. My arms were beginning to bruise from their punches as I closed the door behind me. "I hate you!" I heard. When I didn't respond, they opened the door, slamming it into the previously formed door-handle-shaped hole in the wall. Once, twice, three times, four times, intentionally widening the previously patched cavity. I pulled the door closed and heard a whispered, "I'm making the hole bigger." And I heard chunks of drywall cracking from the wall as dust spread under the door. *This is easy. Loving the kids is the easy part. Easy peasy.*

Peter approaches Jesus as Peter often does—messy and raw and practical. He wants to know, "How many times shall I forgive my brother or sister who sins against me? Up to seven times?" (Matt. 18:21). *This is getting out of hand*, is the suggestion. *I can't just let people walk all over me*, is the implication.

Jesus comes back with a shocking number, somewhere between 77 and 490. The number isn't meant to provide a precise "strike" system for offenses. The number is meant to display that Peter shouldn't be counting at all. The "how many times shall I forgive" number is further fleshed out by Jesus's parable of an unmerciful servant, which further defines the number as more times than you need to be forgiven. In my case, at least, that equates to . . . countless.

This is good news for my children because, as many offenses as my kids may tally up, their in-need-of-forgiveness number is always trumped by my own. My kids aren't the biggest sinners in my house; I am. I'm the chief of them all (1 Tim. 1:15).

Loving my kids through their hard behaviors is anything but "easy peasy, lemon squeezy." It's hard, hard, lemon hard.* But I find the supernatural power to "be kind and compassionate" and "forgiving" to my kids through the punching, kicking, insulting, and drywall-destroying when I remember that I'm called to forgive "just as in Christ God forgave" me (Eph. 4:32).

The forgiveness I've experienced incites the forgiveness I offer. "For if you forgive other people when they sin against you, your heavenly Father will also forgive you," Jesus says (Matt. 6:14). "But if you do not forgive others their sins, your Father will not forgive your sins" (v. 15). This is not so much a command to forgive (and a threat of what will happen if you don't) as it is a descriptor of someone who has been forgiven. The forgiveness we receive becomes not only the motivating factor but also the empowering fuel. Yes, Jesus has forgiven me, so I *should* forgive others; but also, Jesus has forgiven me, so I *can* forgive others.

---

*Yes, of course, I understand that these behaviors are shaped by trauma, but they are also fueled by sin. My kids—and I—are in need of both healing and forgiveness.

Being forgiven transforms me into the kind of person who forgives others.

Like the sinful woman who anointed Jesus's feet with tears and expensive perfume, if we forgive much, we love much (Luke 7:36–50). I have been forgiven so much. When I am in awe of the Jesus who would forgive and love me, I am empowered to forgive and love those around me. "Forgive as the Lord forgave you," Colossians 3:13 commands. I've been forgiven—countless times—with a love that is unconditional and supernatural. This is the kind of forgiveness I'm called to offer to those who sin against me. This is the kind of forgiveness I'm empowered to offer to those who sin against me, including and especially my children.

FURTHER READING

Luke 7:36–50; Psalm 103

5

For you formed my inward parts;
> you knitted me together in my mother's womb.
I praise you, for I am fearfully and wonderfully made.
Wonderful are your works;
> my soul knows it very well.
My frame was not hidden from you,
when I was being made in secret,
> intricately woven in the depths of the earth.
Your eyes saw my unformed substance;
in your book were written, every one of them,
> the days that were formed for me,
> when as yet there was none of them.

Psalm 139:13–16 ESV

I was the foster parent trainer accompanying the staff Child Protective Services (CPS) trainer. This was a recruitment event, which felt kind of gross, but I justified the cringey salesman-like pitch by reminding myself that there are a lot of kids who need good foster parents.

I knew the deck by heart. Everyone paged through the printout while I tried to add some much-needed humanity to the dry presentation. Finally, we arrived at the section about adoption. "How many of you are hoping to adopt out of foster care?" I asked, and nearly every hand jetted into the air. This was the section of the presentation where I veered way off script. "You will see 'foster to adopt' as one of the checkboxes on your application." My voice was monotone, maybe even a little bit annoyed. "You should know that there is no real foster-to-adopt program, as the focus of the whole system is family preservation and reunification. There are three ways to adopt through the foster care system. First, become a traditional foster parent, care for and (most likely) say goodbye to many children, until eventually a child in your home needs an adoptive family. This happens about 25 percent of the time. Second, wait for a worker or another foster parent to connect you to a child who is in a foster home that decides, right before or after termination of parental rights, that they cannot adopt the child, and then welcome the child into your home. This is called a legal-risk placement because there is still no guarantee that this child will need to be adopted." My tone softened. "Or third, adopt a 'waiting child.'"

I don't begrudge the parents who are hoping to adopt, but I want them to understand that foster care is not an adoption agency and that their wish to adopt may actually get in the way of what the system is set up to do. Most of all, I am committed to bringing a level of realism to these recruitment meetings that they typically lack. "Herein lies the most pressing need for adoptive parents," I continued. "There are over one hundred thousand kids in this country just waiting for adoptive homes. Their parents' rights have been stripped by the court, and they are just waiting."

I clicked to the next slide, which read, "Most children available for adoption are over the age of eight or part of a sibling group, and most have significant special needs, including medical and behavioral problems." The sentence blazed on the bright screen, stealing the dignity of these children, categorizing and dehumanizing them with its limiting words. Like an apologetic salesperson waving away a less-than product—*You don't want this old thing*—the unspoken undertones of this slide were, *The ones that are leftover for adoption are the broken ones.*

The slide remained unread on the screen while I spoke slowly. "The children who are waiting for adoptive families are most often described by what you see on the slide. But more than anything you'll read up here, they are beautiful and precious little human lives with stories and hopes and dreams. They are inherently valuable and hold great worth, their lives full of meaning and purpose. They just need a family to say yes to them."

The foundation of foster care must begin and end with this belief: that children are inherently precious, created by God, valuable, and beloved.

When the baby screams and writhes from the pain of detox, *she is precious*. When the toddler finger-paints with poop minutes after a potty break, *he is precious*. When the little girl lies in accusation because of a deep-seated survival mechanism, *she is precious*. When the child with autism cannot speak or make eye contact, *he is precious*. When the teenager sneaks a boy through her bedroom window, searching for the belonging of love, *she is precious*. When the child from trauma cowers in fear or lashes out in rage, *he is precious*.

Every child you care for, every child in foster care, has inherent value, worth, and preciousness as "[God's] workmanship, created in Christ Jesus" (Eph. 2:10 ESV). Each little life was "created . . . in his own image" (Gen. 1:27), reflects something unique about Him as His image bearer, and points to His beauty and worth as a mirror of His glory. In fact, "the kingdom of heaven belongs to such as these" (Matt. 19:14).

> Every child is artfully and lovingly handcrafted by the Creator. Before time began, each child was loved and cherished and planned. All children were on the heart of the Savior as He bled in love. No past abuse, current struggle, or future prognosis; no gender, race, or ethnicity; no medical diagnosis, mental illness, physical handicap, behavioral issue, or educational classification;

no thing, not one thing, *nothing* steals one ounce of the divine image from a child. No label or prefix or description that marks a young soul as "other" can detract from the inherent worth of a child.*

FURTHER READING

PSALM 139

---

*Jamie C. Finn, *Foster the Family: Encouragement, Hope, and Practical Help for the Christian Foster Parent* (Grand Rapids: Baker Books, 2022), 36.

6

He said to me, "My grace is sufficient for you, for my power is made perfect in weakness." Therefore I will boast all the more gladly about my weaknesses, so that Christ's power may rest on me. That is why, for Christ's sake, I delight in weaknesses, in insults, in hardships, in persecutions, in difficulties. For when I am weak, then I am strong.

2 Corinthians 12:9–10

Most nights, I limp to the post-bedtime finish line. The day is long and hard. I wake before dawn, and I then give and go nearly every moment till dark. Night is a land mine of triggers for my kids—fear of isolation and abandonment, hygiene triggers, nighttime monsters (imagined or once very real), darkness and its frightening shadows, anxiety for the next day, the terrifying quiet that invites intrusive thoughts. The good news for me and my children is that it all plays out when I'm at my very best! (In case you struggle with the concept of sarcasm, it is the use of irony for the sake of humor.)

Moms in movies plop on couches melodramatically. Let me tell you, as a real-life post-bedtime couch plopper myself, that there is absolutely no melodrama involved. My body and mind and spirit need a recovery period from the day. The exhaustion is bone deep, *soul* deep.

Paul, we read in 2 Corinthians 12:7, was given a "thorn in [his] flesh, a messenger of Satan, to torment [him]." We're never told what Paul's particular thorn was. I've certainly imagined the form of Paul's thorn before, but I've spent much more time inventorying my own thorns—the things that pierce with discomfort, that debilitate and bring me to the edge of myself.

Now listen, I'm certainly not labeling my beloved and precious children as "thorns" or "messengers of Satan," but I'm also not *not* labeling them those things. Because, I'll tell you what, they have been used to accomplish the very same things in me that Paul's thorns accomplished in him. Paul's thorns—my thorns—were not only from Satan and used for torment; they were also, ultimately, from God and used as a tool.

As Paul wrestled with his thorn, he "pleaded with the Lord to take it away" from him *three* times (v. 8). But God answered him (don't miss the very first miracle of God's plan to meet Paul by casually passing over the fact that He—*God Himself*—spoke to him in his suffering!) with a reminder of His own sufficient grace and perfect power. God used the weakness-inducing thorns to invite Paul to experience Him in a new, fulfilling, and completing way.

I am exhausted. I am so exhausted in every possible way a body and a spirit can be exhausted. So I pray away my exhaustion. I ask Him to take it away, to make it better: *Don't keep me living at the edge of myself, O God. I want a life that is free and full; I want abundance.* And God answers me, as He did Paul, with an invitation: *Then boast in your weakness. Delight in your weakness. Rejoice in coming to the edge of yourself because it is there that I am found.*

Weakness is not sin; it is limitation. It is capacity. It is inherent not-enough-ness. I don't need to confess and repent of not being sufficient in and of myself. That is part of my humanness. I simply need to admit and glory in the fact that I am not God and run to God to find all that I need. I boast in my incompleteness so that I can experience the glory of Christ's power resting upon me.

This changes the paradigm for all of life, especially the hard parts. Insults, hardships, persecutions, difficulties, and weaknesses—they don't need to be avoided, fought against, or prayed away. They can actually be *delighted* in. Because anything that brings me more of God and His all-sufficient grace and perfect power is a gift.

As I write this, it is 1:02 p.m. I've made it through morning wake-ups; the fifteen steps of finding uniforms, diapers, and bottles, getting kids dressed, making lunches and packing backpacks; tears and outbursts; teeth brushing; school drop-offs; rush hour traffic; and a half day of work. The easiest part of the day is behind me, the hardest part still ahead. But I'm not (only) anticipating exhaustion, not (only) aware of my weakness. I am preparing to meet strength—the kind of supernatural, divinely provided strength that is found only in my weakness. When I am weak, then I am strong.

FURTHER READING

Isaiah 40

7

> Therefore, since we have been justified through faith, we have peace with God through our Lord Jesus Christ, through whom we have gained access by faith into this grace in which we now stand. And we boast in the hope of the glory of God. Not only so, but we also glory in our sufferings, because we know that suffering produces perseverance; perseverance, character; and character, hope. And hope does not put us to shame, because God's love has been poured out into our hearts through the Holy Spirit, who has been given to us.
>
> Romans 5:1–5

*A*nswer: Watching an investigator interrogate my forever children about whether or not their mom hurts them. Knowing my child's anxiety is becoming unmanageable because of the chaos of kids in and out of our home. Seeing my children hurt by the damaging trauma behaviors that play out within our home's walls. Hearing my young daughter ask, "Are we ever going to see her again?" after she says goodbye to her foster sister.

I'll take "Things I would have never chosen for my life" for $1,000, Alex.

There's been true suffering I've experienced—we, my family, have experienced—because of foster care. There are so many things I wouldn't have written into my story. So many things that I've tried to pray away and wouldn't have wanted for myself or my kids. I'm guessing it's been the same for you.

This calls into question what we believe about pain. Is it to be avoided always, at all costs? My protective parental reflex answers a resounding "Yes!" But then why would Paul exhort us to "glory in our sufferings" (v. 3)?

Because by God's good design, suffering—especially the kind of suffering that comes from loving and serving and obeying—brings with it a lot of good: "Suffering produces perseverance; perseverance, character; and character, hope. And hope does not put us to shame." (vv. 3–5).

Do you want to know what I do want for myself and my kids? I want character. I want hope. I want to endure hardship with a stick-with-it-ness that comes through a deep-seated trust. I want a nature that is built on integrity and faithfulness and righteousness. I want a faith that knows something to be true and real, even if it is unseen, because of its sureness in the Lord.

The things we pray for ourselves and our kids—things like character and hope—are often forged through the things we pray away—like suffering. I want the long-lasting, deeply rooted fruit that is only plucked from the tree of suffering. But I resent being planted in the soil of hardship. The thing we want to avoid is the thing God is going to use to produce.

The Holy Spirit is able to transform—through God's love—the suffering of this broken world into persevering, character-rich, hope-filled qualities within us and our children. This is glorious, so we are invited to glory in it. We are invited to look past the suffering and toward the eternal benefits that the suffering can accomplish in us—to the extent that we can actually look at the *suffering itself* and rejoice! Our paradigm for pain is turned on its head.

What is our confidence that—and the means by which—the suffering is glorious? The fact that Jesus's death bought us peace with God, purchased us access to an amazing grace, and guarantees that all things—yes, even and especially the suffering—can *only* bring about good in us. The cross is our great guarantee that God does holy work through suffering.

The sufferings of today are sure. But "the sufferings of this present time are not worth comparing with the glory that is to be revealed to us" (8:18 ESV). So it is important to see suffering through eyes of faith. Glory in it and rejoice in what it's accomplishing in you and your family.

FURTHER READING

1 Peter 1:1–9

8

Whatever you do, work heartily, as for the Lord and not for men, knowing that from the Lord you will receive the inheritance as your reward. You are serving the Lord Christ.

Colossians 3:23–24 ESV

I lugged—along with his little body—the monitor that alerted me when his heart stopped beating. I carefully applied leads and snapped on wires. I used coconut oil to gently lift old adhesive from his translucent skin. I bolted from the bed dozens of times each night to the tune of his ear-piercing alarm, which rang with each skipped heartbeat and stopped my heart as well.

A judge decided I wasn't needed anymore. A worker I'd never met picked him up with a "Welp, time to get going." A mom I would never meet left me on read. A child I'd loved, lost sleep for, labored over would never remember me.

You have your own unseen, unappreciated, unthanked moments of foster parenting, I just know it. You've devoted your days to others who—with preoccupied minds or blinded eyes or hardened hearts—see all you do but miss you completely.

I wish I could sit in the corner and watch you walk the miracle of motherhood (and I mean that in the least creepy way possible):

- You speaking patiently to that worker who didn't show up and didn't call. *That is the grace of God at work in you!*
- You looking with eyes of love at the child who screamed, "I hate you!" *That takes an impossible, supernatural kind of love!*

37

- You rocking the baby through the night while the rest of the house sleeps soundly. *The way you serve is beautiful and important!*
- You answering Mom with kindness when she comes at you with accusation. *That is Jesus at work in you!*

I wish I could see and celebrate these things. But I don't have to. Because it is all seen by the Audience of One Himself. "It is the Lord Christ you are serving" (v. 24 ESV), and He misses nothing. Each gentle answer spoken in love, every brave battle for your child's best, the dishes and diapers and dialogues, all the ways you give and serve and love are done not (only) for the faces in front of you but for the Father above you. This is a way you "offer your [body] as a living sacrifice, holy and pleasing to God" in "true and proper worship" (Rom. 12:1).

"God is not unjust; he will not forget your work and the love you have shown him as you have helped his people" (Heb. 6:10). Because He is just, God is *unable* to miss all that you do for Him as you do for others. I hope your people thank you. I hope you are honored and appreciated. But I wouldn't, you know, count on it. So, in everything you do, do it "for the Lord and not for [them]" (Col. 3:23 ESV). His seeing eyes, His just remembrance, His promise to "reward each of us for what we have done" (Rom. 2:6 CEV) are sure.

The hard and the mundane—God sees it all. I wish I could be there cheering you on, but you don't need me. You have the God of the universe watching you, and He doesn't miss a thing. The Audience of One sees all that you do. He applauds it and He will reward it.

FURTHER READING

Psalm 11

9

As [Jesus] approached the town gate, a dead
person was being carried out—the only son
of his mother, and she was a widow. And
a large crowd from the town was with her.
When the Lord saw her, his heart went out to
her and he said, "Don't cry."

Then he went up and touched the bier
they were carrying him on, and the bearers
stood still. He said, "Young man, I say to you,
get up!" The dead man sat up and began to
talk, and Jesus gave him back to his mother.

Luke 7:12–15

---

don't think I had ever heard the word *trauma* before I became a foster parent ten years ago. To be honest, I don't
think I even heard it in my training to become a foster parent ten years ago. I had a vague idea of war vets experiencing
PTSD when they heard loud bangs, but that was about it.

What I've come to learn is that every child touched by foster
care has experienced trauma before *and because of* foster care.
This means that every child who enters my home is coming with
a brain and body and biology that has been altered by the devastating effects of abuse, neglect, and loss.

There are many tools and techniques for playing a part in your
child's healing (and I recommend that you learn them), but healing is a long journey, one without a final and complete (earthly)
destination. This means that, as foster parents, we don't just
need to be equipped for the work ahead of us; we need to be
encouraged by the hope of the Savior who is with us.

This story in Luke 7 provides us with a picture of the Savior's heart for a grieving and desperate mother. There are other stories in the Gospels where women reach out and touch Jesus, cry out to Him, and call Him Lord. In this story, we don't see any of that. This mother is simply walking along in a crowd, hopelessly grieving her child. And the Lord sees her. He sees her, and He sees her loss and suffering, and His heart goes out to her. "When the Lord saw her, his heart went out to her and he said, 'Don't cry'" (v. 13). Jesus approaches this mother, comforts her, and then intervenes in her grief and transforms her story, bringing life where there was once death. After healing her son, He "gave him back to his mother" (v. 15).

In this story, we are given a glimpse into Jesus's motivation for healing this man. The Savior heals the son *because of* His heart for the mother. We know that God is a Healer, but do we remember that it is His compassion for us that drives Him to heal? That He doesn't just act on our behalf but His heart goes out to us? That His heart for us can be what drives Him to intervene in our children's stories and bring healing and life?

The ESV says, "He had compassion on her" (v. 13). I hope you see yourself in the story of this desperate mother because the position of Jesus is the same toward you. His heart goes out to you; He has compassion on you. You may be plodding along, grieving and hopeless. You may be overwhelmed with all the healing that needs to happen in your home. But your Jesus, He sees you and He has compassion. He can intervene on your behalf. He can heal and bring life and transform. But even in the waiting and the wondering, even if He chooses not to, He is present and near, and His heart goes out to you.

FURTHER READING

Luke 5:17–26

10

Do not conform to the pattern of this world, but be transformed by the renewing of your mind. Then you will be able to test and approve what God's will is—his good, pleasing and perfect will.

Romans 12:2

isten, I know this is not unique to me. But I'm just going to need a moment of your compassion and understanding before you nod and tell me that this is just how it's gonna be.

My house never stays clean. Like never. My kid with ADHD is a human Tasmanian devil. Can't find him? Follow the literal Hansel-and-Gretel trail of sock #1 and #2, shoe #1 and #2, sweatshirt (and maybe even pants), basketball, book, stretched laptop cord, and potato chip crumbs to him cuddled up on the couch. When I point out the path of destruction, he quickly apologizes and gladly picks it all up but is certain to do the same again in eleven minutes. And he is just *one* of my six children. I love a neat house, so I am constantly straightening it all, constantly making our little living space as good as new.

Here's the thing about making something new: As soon as something is made new, it immediately begins the process of becoming old again—from our living rooms to our thought lives.

Our minds become my ADHD son–level chaotic and cluttered when left to themselves. Fears, desires, judgments, and what-ifs will take over—and foster parenting is rife with all of them. I've imagined kids dead or adopted, depending on the

41

situation. I've filled in the gaps of family tales and trees with the least generous of assumptions. I've concocted make-believe that leads me to the depths of despair or the heights of happiness, but never to reality. This is why the Bible calls me to renew my mind.

Mind renewing is the practice of taking "captive every thought to make it obedient to Christ" (2 Cor. 10:5). It's taking "whatever is true, whatever is noble, whatever is right, whatever is pure, whatever is lovely, whatever is admirable—if anything is excellent or praiseworthy—[and] think[ing] about such things" (Phil. 4:8).

The process of renewing your mind is perpetual, constant, and on repeat. It's a day-in, day-out, moment-by-moment practice that takes faith and faithfulness.

But the promised return is worth the hard work: transformation. The patterns of worldly foster parenting are insidious: fear, control, envy, manipulation, anxiety. These worldly patterns tempt us to conform to them with their oh-so-believable lies about our lives and our God. But we can rid our minds of their oldness—clear the cobwebs and scrub the corners—and be transformed.

The transforming, new kind of thinking outlined in Philippians 4:8 might seem like wishful, delusional idealism. Maybe you don't see "right" or "lovely" playing out in your life or in your kids' stories, and so it feels impossible to set your mind on it. You know as well as I do that the "power of positive thinking" is powerless to change your circumstances.

It might be time for you to look away from your circumstances completely—and to your God. Where can I find truth, nobility, righteousness, purity, loveliness, admirability, excellence, and praiseworthiness in the midst of an unjust system and a broken family? In the God above it all. So, I don't bury my head in the sand; I lift my eyes. And when I renew my mind and set it on Him, I am transformed.

FURTHER READING

Romans 12

11

Cast your burden on the LORD,
and he will sustain you.

Psalm 55:22 ESV

As soon as she got in the car, I could see she wasn't okay. "Can I have a friend over?" she asked.

"I would like for you to have a friend over soon; let's try to find a day when they can because today we have other plans," I responded, eggshells cracking beneath my feet.

I'm good friends with zero to sixty. This was more like zero to one thousand. This kiddo began lashing out immediately—verbally and physically—growling, screaming, punching the window, kicking at seats and siblings. "We're only a few minutes from home, everyone; it's okay," I said as I made eye contact with each of the other kids in the rearview mirror, desperate to provide some small comfort in the midst of this chaos.

We ran into the house, and I handed the littles to my teenager, who sprang into action. "Lock yourself in my room and play worship music—loudly," I said.

Over the next hour, I heard animalistic screams and piercing insults. I saw a huge hole bored into a recently patched wall and my computer thrown down the stairs. I felt dozens of slaps and punches across my arms and legs. I felt—with a deeper sting than the welts forming on my skin—heartbroken, hopeless, afraid, exhausted.

My burdens—my sadness for this child's brokenness, my anxiety for my other children, my helplessness to create healing, my weariness of the constant struggle, my fear for the future—are heavy. I simply cannot carry them. They are too heavy for my aching arms and heart.

But I am invited to cast them on my God. Hunched and overwhelmed by the burdens I carry, I release them into the arms and hands of my God. These arms "[stretched] out the heavens" (Isa. 40:22) and "spread out the earth" (Ps. 136:6). These hands "measured the waters in [their] hollow" and "marked off the heavens with [their] span" (Isa. 40:12 ESV). Most unbelievable of all, these hands hold us within them (John 10:29) and have our names engraved upon them (Isa. 49:16). They are secure. They are capable. They are loving.

Psalm 55:22 doesn't say that when we release our burdens to God, He will remove them. It doesn't say He will eliminate them or even intervene in them. It doesn't say anything about the burdens at all. It says that He will sustain us. He will carry us. He will provide all that we need. He will supply and strengthen.

Partnering with our kids in the healing of their brains and bodies, participating in the stories of our kids' families, and infiltrating a broken system are long-haul, substantial kinds of burdens that take a divine, supernatural kind of sustaining. That sustenance is available to us. All we have to do is bring our burdens before Him and cast them upon Him. And He will sustain us.

FURTHER READING

Matthew 11:25–30

12

> Therefore, as God's chosen people, holy and dearly loved, clothe yourselves with compassion, kindness, humility, gentleness and patience. . . . And over all these virtues put on love, which binds them all together in perfect unity.
>
> Colossians 3:12, 14

I run a business that benefits children entering foster care and creates T-shirts and products catered to foster parents. We create beautiful designs with inspiring phrases like "Love Is Brave" and "Foster Love" and "Show Love." Our mission is to make clothing that encourages foster parents for the journey of foster parenting.

You want to know some platitudes about foster parenting that are just as true as those above but that you're never going to find on a T-shirt?

Love is brave enough to endure hearing "I hate you. You're not my real mom."

Foster love = patching holes in the wall from last night's three-hour meltdown.

Show love to the mom whose kid is crying in your arms because she didn't show up for her visit.

It might be radical love—for God, for others—that pulls you into foster parenting, but that love is sure to have a head-on collision with unlovely at some point.

I have fallen head over heels in love with the kids who've entered my home through foster care. I deeply love my forever children and would do anything for them. I have profound compassion for the struggling parents of my kids. And as much as each of these things is true, they also are often *not*. I struggle to feel connection, have affection, and show patience. I fail at showing compassion, and I come with pride. I parent with ungentle and unkind words and actions.

Even in this mission that is motivated and driven by love and compassion, I too often live it out without love and compassion. That's why I love the language of Colossians 3:12 and 14. It assumes our natural state is not as it should be: namely, naked.

"Clothe yourselves," commands verse 12, and "put on," encourages verse 14. These verses acknowledge that love is not something that you "fall into," as culture would have us believe. They remind us that compassion, kindness, humility, gentleness, and patience are not personality traits that you're born with or without.

Rather, we must make the active choice to love. Love is a verb, something we do, something we must take the action of putting on. We must *clothe* ourselves in the Christlike qualities of loving foster parenting that don't come naturally to us.

We put off apathy and put on compassion, put off bitterness and put on kindness, put off arrogance and put on humility, put off harshness and put on gentleness, put off impatience and put on patience.

Why and how? Because we are God's people, which means that, at once, we are called to obedience *and* we are equipped by His power. The call to love is a command. But we must not forget who this command is directed to: those "who are beloved of God" (Rom. 1:7 NASB). As those who have been dearly loved by the Savior, we have been changed into people who have the

Savior's supernatural power to love (2 Cor. 5:14)—even and especially the unlovely and the hard to love.

And so we love—like putting on a favorite old T-shirt with an encouraging slogan—by pulling our arms through it, clothing ourselves in it, and putting it on.

FURTHER READING

1 Peter 4

13

May the God of hope fill you with all joy and peace as you trust in him, so that you may overflow with hope by the power of the Holy Spirit.

Romans 15:13

---

remember the parking lot I pulled into to take the call. "He's going to go back to Mom in a week," the worker said nonchalantly, as if she thought that this was what should happen, as if she hadn't just told me a day ago that—in her opinion—if he went home, his life was at risk.

It felt like a punch in the gut. I know that's an expression people throw around—"punch in the gut"—but this felt like an actual blow to my midsection. My stomach ached with emptiness—one part rage, one part sorrow. I didn't cry; I didn't call anyone. I just started my car, drove on autopilot, and nursed my aching belly.

I'm going to call the worker, and I'm going to tell her that this is wrong and— No, I'm not even going to give any explanation; I'm just going to call and say, "I quit. I am no longer a foster parent. I quit."

I swerved into the first convenience store I came to and beelined through the doors and to the exact place I knew they would be—"cakes" covered in pink-tinted "coconut" and filled with "cream." I needed something to fill this emptiness in my gut, something to overwhelm the anger and anxiety. I sat in the car and stuffed them into my mouth in too few bites. Guess what? It didn't work.

As a foster parent, I face so many emptying things—broken promises, unjust decisions, struggling children, tumultuous upheavals—that I am regularly brought to my knees in utter desperation. Sometimes I attempt to fill myself with lesser things (case in point: the "cream"-filled "cakes"), but these gods always pale before the Filler Himself.

Idolatry doesn't look quite like it used to, which makes it all the more insidious. I am not tempted to bow down to statues of silver or gold, but I am tempted to "[exchange] the truth about God for a lie, and [worship and serve] created things rather than the Creator" (1:25). I am tempted to find pleasure or comfort or *hope* in a created source. The god of convenience-store cake, sure. Also, the god of my children, my family, my happily ever after. Or the god of mind-numbing scrolling (escape), the god of "let's go on an adventure" (pleasure), the god of analyzing on repeat (control). These false gods offer counterfeits with their insidious lies and steal with their feeble schemes. They never truly deliver the hope they promise, and they lead us away from the true Source of hope.

"The God of hope" is His name. Hope—a confident expectation of the good that is certain to arrive—is such a defining trait of who He is that it becomes a surname of sorts. And it's this God of hope whom we can come to, with expectant, hopeful trust, for filling. It is He who can submerge us under the depths of His great joy and peace.

When I am emptied by my anger and anxiety, I need something greater to swell into those spaces and overwhelm them completely. What begins with confession and repentance and killing idols leads to peace and joy. The peace He offers is a peace that "surpasses all understanding" (Phil. 4:7 ESV)— a peace that makes no sense. The joy He gives is a completing (John 15:11), strengthening (Neh. 8:10) kind of joy that no one can take (John 16:22). His peace and joy redefine my reality completely, and when I place my trust in them—in Him—I am filled to overflowing with no space left for the competing, lesser gods.

The power of the Holy Spirit is a supernatural kind of power that fills to overflowing. My access key to an overflowing, Spirit-filled love and hope and peace is simple: trusting that He can, believing that He will, and watching Him deliver.

FURTHER READING

Exodus 20:1–20; Galatians 5

14

If someone slaps you on one cheek, turn to them the other also. If someone takes your coat, do not withhold your shirt from them. Give to everyone who asks you, and if anyone takes what belongs to you, do not demand it back.

Luke 6:29–30

The world talks about relationships like they're a buffet line. *Take what you want and leave the rest*, it offers. *If you're unhappy, then move on and live your truth*, it directs. Every fifth Instagram post I come across is about cutting out toxic people, dropping unfulfilling relationships, and only surrounding yourself with people who "protect your peace."

Let me put this as delicately as I can: These ideas are anti-gospel trash. The gospel destroys every rational, worldly paradigm for relationship and calls us to an unreasonable, reckless kind of love. Following Jesus completely redefines everything about our relationships—the way we think, talk, act, forgive, even the people we are in relationship with—and entering foster care provides the sanctifying space to practice this upside-down kind of living and loving.

"If someone slaps you on one cheek, turn to them the other also. If someone takes your coat, do not withhold your shirt from them" (v. 29). Is this passage encouraging physically abusive relationships and theft? No, absolutely not. Is it calling Christians to an unreasonable, irrational, self-sacrificial kind of love? Absolutely. We can't lean on the foolish wisdom of the world (1 Cor.

3:19) to define what our love should look like as foster parents. We must go to the Source for the 180 relational paradigm of the gospel.

The world says, "Drop people who don't treat you as you deserve." The gospel says, "Love your enemies, do good to those who hate you" (Luke 6:27).

The world says, "You have to stand up for yourself or they'll never learn." The gospel says, "Repay evil with blessing" (1 Pet. 3:9).

The world says, "If they let you down, don't waste your energy on them." The gospel says, "If your enemy is hungry, feed him; if he is thirsty, give him something to drink" (Rom. 12:20).

The world says, "Fool me once, shame on you; fool me twice, shame on me." The gospel says, "Love your enemies and pray for those who persecute you" (Matt. 5:44).

Can I be honest for a moment? I find it particularly hard to love my kids' parents and families. My protective, mama-bear instincts collide with my judgmental, self-righteous ideas and lead me to feel something closer to apathy or hatred than the love I'm called to. My kids' parents have done (or not done) things that have hurt the children I love, that have caused brokenness and trauma that pervade every part of their lives. Has the behavior of my kids' parents *merited* honor and blessing? No. Do they *deserve* love and forgiveness? Definitely not.

But thank God that gospel love doesn't rely on our merits, doesn't wait for us to deserve it. When I was sick (Mark 2:17) and enslaved (John 8:34), hostile to God (Rom. 8:7) and dead in sin (Eph. 2:1), it was then that God loved me, there that Jesus laid down His life for me in love (John 15:13). I was not only lost (Luke 15:32) and wandering, I was "foolish, disobedient, led astray, [a slave] to various passions and pleasures, passing [my] days in malice and envy, hated by others and hating" (Titus 3:3

ESV). And in this state, in my utter unworthiness and desperation, God saw me and placed His love on me. And His love was not left untouched by my brokenness. He didn't watch from afar; He put on my skin and took on my sin and took the punishment for it all. His love for me came at a great cost to Himself. It cost Him His very life.

This is why and *this is how* we are called to a different kind of love than the shallow, self-protective love that the world sponsors. "Just as I have loved you," commands Jesus, "you also are to love one another" (John 13:34 ESV). "Just as I have loved you" is a daunting, radical call to a love that is unconditional and reckless, that gives itself, that lays down its life. And it calls me to—and empowers me to live out—a higher and holier, dying kind of love for those who are just as deserving of it as I am. Namely, not at all.

Note: Let me be clear—God hates abuse in all its forms. Luke 6:29–30 does not condone abuse and should never be twisted into a mandate for victims to endure abuse. If you are in an abusive relationship of any kind, please reach out to someone for immediate protection and care. In all cases of violence, I would encourage you to talk to both your church leaders for care and the authorities for protection and justice.

FURTHER READING

1 Corinthians 13

15

I remember my affliction and my wandering,
   the bitterness and the gall.
I well remember them,
   and my soul is downcast within me.
Yet this I call to mind
   and therefore I have hope:
Because of the LORD's great love we are not consumed,
   for his compassions never fail.
They are new every morning;
   great is your faithfulness.
I say to myself, "The LORD is my portion;
   therefore I will wait for him." . . .
Though he brings grief, he will show compassion,
   so great is his unfailing love.
For he does not willingly bring affliction
   or grief to anyone.

Lamentations 3:19–24, 32–33

She wasn't ready. Everyone knew she wasn't ready—wasn't ready to be on her own, wasn't ready to parent on a day-to-day basis—but they sent him home anyway. "We can't build a case for termination of parental rights, and our clock has run out, so what else can we do?" was the simple explanation. I believe in reunification. I fight for it and pray for it and work toward it. But when it happens and it shouldn't, when it happens and a child's safety is at risk, I lament it.

I'm a recovering "just look on the bright side" kind of Christian. I spent most of my life understanding verses like "rejoice always" (1 Thess. 5:16) to mean that there was no space in the

Christian's life for anything but constant happiness. I didn't understand godly grief, and I hadn't learned the biblical practice of lament.

Lament is a kind of prayer that we didn't learn in Sunday school. It's a prayer of pain, brought in faith to the Father. It's a tearful, kicking-and-screaming kind of prayer that rails against the broken, upside-down-ness of this world. It says, "This isn't supposed to be like this," but, rather than wallowing in hopeless-ness, cries out in a holy union of pain and petition and surrender.

Don't be like me and let "Smile, Jesus loves you" posters lead you to believe faithfulness always wears a grin. We see lament all throughout Scripture. David wrote a whole book of confused and heartbroken poems, and he was "a man after [God's] own heart" (Acts 13:22). Job grieved and mourned and questioned God but through it all had only "spoken the truth about [Him]" (Job 42:7). Jeremiah gave us five chapters of desperate lam-entations, and God Himself had "reached out his hand and touched [Jeremiah's] mouth and said to [him], 'I have put my words in your mouth'" (Jer. 1:9). And even Jesus, the perfect Son of God, confessed His soul was "overwhelmed with sorrow to the point of death" (Matt. 26:38) and "being in agony . . . prayed more earnestly [until] his sweat became like great drops of blood falling down to the ground" (Luke 22:44 ESV).

In each of these cases, we see men of God (and even the Son of God) in deep grief and sorrow, bringing their words—in songs and poems, lamentations, and bloody, sweaty prayers—to God in faith. They air their sorrows, bring their requests, and then finally, ultimately declare their trust.

This is the model of godly lament we can follow. It sets up camp in the tension between "This is not good" and "You are good." It screams out in anger and confusion, "Children shouldn't be hurt. Families shouldn't be torn apart. Hearts shouldn't be broken," and then asks God, who is above it all, to intervene, and finally surrenders in faith to whatever good He has ordained.

As you walk through injustice and suffering, reject the idea that holiness requires happiness. Cry out to your God with honest heartbreak and pray faith-filled prayers of lament.

FURTHER READING

Lamentations 3

16

> The righteousness of God has been made known. . . . Given through faith in Jesus Christ to all who believe. . . . For all have sinned and fall short of the glory of God, and all are justified freely by his grace through the redemption that came by Christ Jesus. God presented Christ as a sacrifice of atonement, through the shedding of his blood—to be received by faith.
>
> Romans 3:21–25

There are two categories of "mom fails." The first is the kind we accept and celebrate. They're the "I'm just like you" confessions of messy mom life that merit laugh emojis and raised hands of solidarity. As a scatterbrained mom of six with too much on her plate, I've got a long laundry list of these. Then there is the other kind. They're the "What if anyone found out?" moments of shame that peel back deep layers of guilt and remorse. As a sinful and selfish mom who struggles with anger and arrogance, I've got a list of these too. Screaming at screaming kids, shooting dirty looks, spewing cutting sarcasm, withdrawing my affection. I have had many moments of unspeakable failures in motherhood. These written here are the speakable ones.

It's easy as a foster parent to talk about the brokenness of the system, the families, the parents, and the kids like they're "out there" kinds of problems, like we are not touched by the same brokenness ourselves. "None is righteous, no, not one; no one understands; no one seeks for God. All have turned aside" is the tragic diagnosis of Romans 3:10–12 (ESV). It's not just "them," it's "all," and it's not just "all," it's *me*.

I sin out loud in ways that are obviously wrong and wicked. But there are also the quiet—and just as insidious—sins of my heart. I judge and criticize parents. I doubt God's goodness and give in to fear. I want my own will over His. I resent the good gifts He's given me. I elevate my limited understanding over His infinite wisdom. I put my hope in lesser, failing gods. And the sentence for this sin? The most devastating news possible: separation between me and my God (Isa. 59:2).

The bad news must precede the good news—the best news of all. "While we were still sinners, Christ died for us," and now we can be "justified by his blood" and "saved from God's wrath through him" (Rom. 5:8–9). This is an impossible kind of gift, and it only has to be received. I can't earn it, and there's nothing I could do to deserve it. "Repent therefore, and turn back, that your sins may be blotted out" (Acts 3:19) is the simple and glorious call of the gospel.

The wages of my sin were devastatingly costly for Him, but His free gift to me is eternal life in Jesus (Rom. 6:23). And "there is now no condemnation" (8:1)—absolutely *no condemnation*—and I don't have to hide in shame. My sin tells me to cover and protect. *No one—not even Jesus—could love me as I am.* But when "we confess our sins, he is faithful and just to forgive us our sins and to cleanse us" (1 John 1:9 ESV). All that's left for us is the freedom of forgiveness and the joy of being made clean.

The infection of sin pervades every corner of my heart and my foster parenting, but it does not have the final word. Repent, believe, and receive is the invitation of the gospel. Oh, how glorious it is to be forgiven! Oh, how sweet it is to be free!

FURTHER READING

Romans 5

17

Jesus, delivered up according to the definite plan and foreknowledge of God, you crucified and killed by the hands of lawless men.

Acts 2:23 ESV

Remember I told you that court was coming up soon? Well, it was yesterday, and I found out today that baby Daniel is going to be going home in a few days."

We have regular check-ins with our (forever) kids about the direction of our (foster) kids' cases. We want to protect them from being flung up and down every bump of the foster care roller coaster, but we don't want them to be blindsided by an abrupt change in our family. So we do our best to walk the delicate line of sharing information. Sometimes we're blindsided ourselves, though, and there's no preparation we could've offered.

"What? No! Mom, please!" my daughter cried in protest.

"Baby, you know that I don't get to decide these things; the judge does. The judge is sending him home to his mom. It's God's plan for him to go home now."

"Well, was it the judge or was it God?" she challenged.

"Well, um . . . it was . . . both" was the best I could come up with.

"But you said his mom still wasn't healthy! You said she wasn't ready to take care of him yet!"

"Well, the judge disagrees and thinks that she's healthy enough, and so we have to try to trust God," I answered.

"But does *God* disagree and think she's healthy enough? You said that this is God's plan, that we should trust Him. If she's not healthy and God is the one who's sending him home, then why would God do that?"

Oof. My daughter asked aloud the questions that I'm sometimes too afraid to wrestle through—the ones that are so hard that to spend too much time contemplating them brings up other, even harder questions.

How do you explain to your young child—or to your own heart—that you believe seemingly contradictory ideas at the same time? That you don't know where one truth ends and one begins, but you believe them both simultaneously and believe that they are not, in fact, in opposition?

Like, for example (and please spend the time looking up these references and wrestling through them—don't take my word for it!), that:

- Judges make the wrong decisions, but God directs the hearts of leaders to accomplish His plans (Luke 18:1–8; Matt. 27:23–24; Prov. 21:1; Rom. 13:1).
- God hates when people hurt each other—when parents hurt their children—but He ordains everything to bring about His good will (Prov. 6:16–19; Gen. 50:20; Job 1:21; 2:10).
- People do the wrong thing and get away with it, but God's perfect justice will always win (Job 21:7–15; Eccles. 3:17; Isa. 61:8).

A powerful example of the tension between the evil and injustice of people and the sovereignty of God is found in Acts 2. In the first "church sermon" ever preached, Peter both condemns his listeners and exalts the sovereignty of God in one sentence: "This Jesus, delivered up according to the definite plan and foreknowledge of God, you crucified and killed by the hands of lawless men" (v. 23 ESV).

He claims two seemingly contradictory things in just a few words, that Jesus was both

- "delivered" by God, according to His "definite plan" and "foreknowledge," *and*
- "crucified" by "you" and "killed by the hands of lawless men."

Was it that God "so loved the world, that he *gave* his only Son" (John 3:16, emphasis mine)? Or that "the chief priests and our rulers *delivered* Him to the sentence of death, and *crucified* Him" (Luke 24:20 NASB, emphasis mine)? The answer: Yes.

The brutal murder of the Son of God is the most evil act ever perpetrated by any person. As the only perfect person ever to live, as God in the flesh, His crucifixion is the single greatest act of injustice on this earth. Yet would any of us question that God ordained, allowed, and had a very, very good plan in this evil act executed by "wicked hands" (Acts 2:23 KJV)?

There is no simple answer to the "Is it God or the judge?" question or many of the other questions that beg "Where is God and is He good?" inherent to foster care. I can't offer my daughter a wrapped-up-pretty-with-a-bow conclusion. But I can comfort her—and my own heart—with the truth that, in some mysterious way, God sovereignly allows what seems as though it could only be bad to bring about His good. His sovereignty is a mystery that I can't fully understand. But when I surrender to it, I find the great hope and peace that is found in knowing the God who is too great to be fully known.

FURTHER READING

Romans 9 and the verses listed above

18

So we fix our eyes not on what is seen, but on what is unseen, since what is seen is temporary, but what is unseen is eternal.

2 Corinthians 4:18

I drove him home, and this time, it was *home* home. Not home for a visit, not home for a weekend, this time it was home forever. We knocked on the door and no one opened. So we knocked again and again. As he ran to the back window and banged there, I watched a neighborhood woman stumble out of the passenger seat of a parked car. She wore a black sequined dress, and her head leaned lifelessly to one side like a character from *The Walking Dead*.

"Let's sit in the car and try to call," I suggested. I called Mom's phone a dozen times. She didn't pick up. One teenage boy ran next to the car, joined soon by a second, third, fourth. They gathered and talked and then, in a moment, sprinted around the corner. *It is nine o'clock on a Sunday morning. How is all of this going on at nine o'clock on a Sunday morning?*

We called again, knocked again, and finally, after a half hour of trying, I looked at him. "I'm not sure what else to do right now, buddy. I think we should probably go back home—to my home—and see if we can get ahold of your mom later."

"Okay," he answered quietly.

The phone rang as we drove home silently. "Hello?" he said, as I handed him the phone, wanting to save Mom the embarrassment of having to explain to me.

"Baby, I'm sorry," I overheard. "I went to the Phillies game last night, and I stayed at my friend's house. I forgot you were coming. I'm not sure where your daddy is. I'll give you the address; just come here."

"I'm glad we heard from her! Do you know this friend?" I asked as I turned the car around. "Do you feel safe there?"

"My mom's there," was his simple response. We parked the car, and I unloaded his things. I told him that if he ever needed anything at all, he could text me. Then I said goodbye and hugged him. Mom popped her head out the door, and he pulled away.

"Thank you," she said without a smile and pulled him inside. I drove away and never heard from him again.

For three months, this child's every need was my first priority. And then, in a moment, he was gone. No tearful homecoming, no big thank-you speech, and (in my mind, at least) no real impact made. What was the point of giving this child so much of my time, my heart, *myself* for him to just leave before any real change could take place in his family, before any meaningful change could happen in his mind or heart or life? The energy and emotion we had spent on him felt meaningless, our impact worthless.

But what I can see and measure is not all there is. This is why, as believers, "we fix our eyes not on what is seen, but on what is unseen, since what is seen is temporary, but what is unseen is eternal" (2 Cor. 4:18). The "seen" of foster care—the temporary, the loss, the injustice, the brokenness—is glaring. It threatens to overwhelm our eyes and our hearts with its confined visibility. But above what we see—and even more real—is an entire "heavenly realm" (Eph. 2:6).

As I spend up my days in the mundaneness and seeming meaninglessness of foster care, God is accomplishing eternal purposes and plans. He is writing stories for lives to be changed, for the trajectory of families to be altered, for communities to be impacted, for His kingdom to come to earth as it is in heaven.

God is doing things in and through our families that aren't visible with eyes, things that—this side of heaven—we will probably never see. But it doesn't mean we don't look. We "set [our] hearts on things above" (Col. 3:1), looking past the obviously discouraging and limited view of what is done and left undone—and to Him. We don't define success in earthly terms of results or outcomes. We faithfully sow and serve and entrust it all to Him "who is able to do immeasurably more than all we ask or imagine" (Eph. 3:20) and far more than we can see.

When you're discouraged by what you see, when you're questioning your impact, when you're wondering if all of this is worth it, "set your hearts on things above, where Christ is" (Col. 3:1), and fix your eyes on what is eternal (2 Cor. 4:18).

FURTHER READING

2 Corinthians 4

19

And he humbled you and let you hunger and fed you with manna, which you did not know, nor did your fathers know, that he might make you know that man does not live by bread alone, but man lives by every word that comes from the mouth of the LORD.

Deuteronomy 8:3 ESV

I have six kids, ages three months to fourteen years old. Getting out of the house each morning for school and work is a Herculean feat. I get out of bed at 5:00 a.m., three hours before we have to leave for the day. My morning includes giving one bottle, changing two diapers, setting out three uniforms, packing four lunches, reminding five kids to brush their teeth, and getting six kids into the car. Every single night, when I set my alarm for 4:45 a.m., I think, *I can't do this again.* And every single morning, the grace to do it all again is there waiting for me.

I am forgetful, just like God's people have always been. We all know the stories—God's people, enslaved in Egypt and crying out to Him. He miraculously rescues them (see burning bushes, water turned into blood, and dry roads through walls of seas) and promises to bring them to a land He has chosen for them—a good land flowing with milk and honey. Almost immediately, they begin to complain. "If only we had died by the LORD's hand in Egypt! There we sat around pots of meat and ate all the food we wanted, but you have brought us out into this desert to starve this entire assembly to death" (Exod.

16:3). I think God should've struck them down right then and there (though I am personally grateful He is forbearing with His people's forgetting and grumbling)—*I did all this for you, and now you're reminiscing after slavery and wishing for death?* But He is merciful. "Then the LORD said to Moses, 'I will rain down bread from heaven for you. The people are to go out each day and gather enough for that day. In this way I will test them and see whether they will follow my instructions'" (v. 4).

God had a plan. He was going to literally rain food down from heaven. "It was like coriander seed, white, and the taste of it was like wafers made with honey" (v. 31 ESV). The people called it manna, which literally meant "What is it?" and is just the most hilariously uncreative naming of a thing I've ever heard. God would provide it each and every morning, and all they had to do was collect what He had provided. It was a plan to feed them, certainly, but He had a deeper intention.

God provided for their physical need of hunger, but the daily manna rainfall was about more than just their bellies. It was about their hearts. "He humbled [them] and let [them] hunger and fed [them] with manna" (Deut. 8:3 ESV) to teach them that their very lives were dependent on Him and Him alone.

The manna would melt away with the sunrise and spoil with the sunfall. They couldn't hoard, they couldn't stockpile, they couldn't in any way multiply the manna to make themselves less dependent on the Manna Sender. All they could do was wait, wake, and anticipate the goodness and provision of their God, day after day after day. He could've fed them by any multitude of methods. He mercifully chose to feed them in a way that tore down their reliance on themselves and built their trust in Him.

Maybe your mornings are like mine and you need the supernatural strength of God just to get out the door. Or maybe it's not the tasks of the morning but the feelings you'll face with the rising sun—the anxieties or heartaches, the frightening or the unknown. Whatever it is that you'll meet with the dawn, don't forget that "His mercies never come to an end; they are new every morning" (Lam. 3:22–23 ESV). Don't forget that the manna is waiting for you—His promise to sustain you, to provide for you, and to keep you dependent on Him.

FURTHER READING

Deuteronomy 8

20

Immediately Jesus made the disciples get
into the boat and go on ahead of him to the
other side, while he dismissed the crowd.
After he had dismissed them, he went up
on a mountainside by himself to pray.

Matthew 14:22–23

"Keep saying yes." I have a T-shirt with this phrase across it. In fact, I created the T-shirt with this phrase across it. I stand behind the message—the inspirational words to encourage foster parents to keep going when it's hard, when there's heartbreak, when there's loss. But it would probably be appropriate to also create a T-shirt with the less heartwarming but just as important message, "Time to say no."

In my work, I've seen many foster parents who should've said no. Some whose licensing and training workers should've said no—on their behalf—from the outset. Some who should've done more growing or learning or establishing before saying yes. Mostly, I've seen those who are great people and great foster parents who have so much to offer kids and just need to say no *for now*.

We read in Matthew 14:16–21 about Jesus famously feeding the five thousand—five thousand people "he had compassion on" (v. 14), five thousand people He saw and loved enough to bring His miracles and message to—one of the most famous stories of Jesus meeting the physical and spiritual needs of desperate people. And then? He immediately dismisses them and goes off to pray (vv. 22–23). This is one of many times like it when people were gathering around Him and "He gave orders to depart to the other side of the sea" (8:18 NASB), or "He entered a house and did not want anyone to know it" (Mark 7:24).

But what about the people and their needs, Jesus? Certainly—among this crowd—there were the sick who needed healing and the weak who needed helping and, of course, the sinners who needed saving. Yet it seems as though Jesus sent many people off without completely healing, fulfilling, or delivering every one of them.

Should we gather from this text that we should say no to meeting others' needs in order to spend prolonged time in prayer? Maybe. But more than that, I think it's a reminder that even the Savior did not meet every need of every person He came across. And we are no Savior.

It is uniquely challenging to receive an actual phone call about an actual human life and say, "No, I will not help this person." But as limited beings, we simply cannot help every person who needs us. And we have the example of Jesus, who, even with His limitless power, did not help every person who needed Him.

What does it take for us as foster parents to say no when our bleeding hearts and guilt-ridden heads want only ever to say yes? I believe it takes the humility of remembering and acknowledging that we are not God and cannot meet everyone's needs. As well as the trust and faith *in* God that He *is* and *can*. "The God who made the world and everything in it . . . is not served by human hands, as if he needed anything" (Acts 17:24–25). It is a gift that God often uses *us* to be His earthly hands and feet in the lives of those in need. But these "human hands" of ours are simply means He chooses to wield, and He has countless other methods at His fingers—natural and supernatural alike.

The longer I'm at this, the deeper I've come to understand that it takes a lot of faith to say yes, and it often takes just as much faith to say no.

FURTHER READING

Psalms 3–4

21

The LORD is my strength and my shield;
my heart trusts in him, and he helps me.

Psalm 28:7

What if he gets hurt during the overnight visit? What if she's still this violent when she's an adult? What if Mom calls CPS on us? What if she gets pregnant? What if the abusive boyfriend moves in once the worker closes the case? What if the lawyer lies again? What if the next suicide attempt is successful? What if the judge awards custody to the great-aunt across the country? What if he acts out his abuse on my other children? What if Mom relapses?

Did I list your what-if? Do you have others?

We watch and walk such frightening paths. We've seen how the broken family and the broken system breed brokenness, and our brains construct logical questions: *What if this? What if that? What if not?* Our what-ifs aren't irrational or unusual. They're the natural overflow of the suffering we see.

But peace isn't found in concocting answers to our what-if questions. It's found in asking another question completely. My friend Jason Johnson taught me the power of asking, "What else is true?" Yes, it's true that this scary and sad thing might happen. But what else is true? Yes, it's true that this thing we're walking through is incredibly hard. But what else is true?

What else is true? To this question there is always some bold and beautiful answer about God that changes everything. Knowing and remembering big truths about God builds the kind of heart-steadying faith that leads us to say, "My heart trusts in him, and he helps me" (Ps. 28:7).

"When I am afraid, I put my trust in you," David wrote. "In God, whose word I praise—in God I trust and am not afraid" (56:3–4). David had many reasons to be afraid—attempted murder, betrayal, enemies within and outside his kingdom—and he could've been plagued by what-ifs. But *What if* . . . can be overwhelmed by *He is* . . . And David knew many grand and glorious truths about God. He penned a whole book of them:

> For you, O Lord, are good and forgiving,
>> abounding in steadfast love to all who call upon you.
>>> (86:5 ESV)

> The Lord reigns. . . .
> Your statutes, Lord, stand firm. (93:1, 5)

> The Lord is compassionate and gracious,
> Slow to anger and abounding in lovingkindness.
>> (103:8 NASB)

> The Lord watches over you. . . .

> The Lord will keep you from all harm—
>> he will watch over your life. (121:5, 7)

> He determines the number of the stars;
>> he gives to all of them their names.
> Great is our Lord, and abundant in power;
>> his understanding is beyond measure. (147:4–5 ESV)

What is the gospel hope that you can hold on to? Which comforts of His character can you cling to? Make them mantras that you grip your heart around. Memorize them and speak them to yourself and others. Answer "What else is true?" with truth from His Word. Hide His Word in your heart that—when you're tempted to fear or to forget—you might not sin against Him (119:11).

Peace isn't found in ignoring the frightening realities that surround us; it's found in seeing them, then looking to Him. We don't put our heads in the sand; we lift them heavenward. So "lift up [your] eyes to the hills," friend, because your "help comes from the LORD, who made heaven and earth" (121:1–2 ESV).

So, as the frightening questions of foster parenting tempt your heart to ask, "What if?" respond with "What else is true?" and then remind yourself of the many true things about your God, anchor your heart in trust of Him, and He will help you.

FURTHER READING

Psalm 121 (Challenge: memorize one of the verses above or another short psalm that answers your most pressing what-if question.)

22

Do not repay evil with evil or insult with insult.
On the contrary, repay evil with blessing, because
to this you were called so that you may inherit a
blessing. . . .

> "For the eyes of the Lord are on the righteous
>   and his ears are attentive to their prayer,
> but the face of the Lord is against those who
>   do evil."

Who is going to harm you if you are eager to
do good? But even if you should suffer for what is
right, you are blessed. "Do not fear their threats;
do not be frightened. But in your hearts revere
Christ as Lord.

1 Peter 3:9, 12–15

I handled the visit drop-offs and pickups, due mostly to my
flexible schedule. But my husband, Alan, offered to do this
one. It was no big deal. He knew Mom well and had an
open and warm relationship with her. But when he arrived back
home with our (foster) daughter in tow, I could read the anxiety
on his face. "What? What's wrong?" I asked.

"Dad was there," he said. Dad—who I had met only once in a
prison visitation room—was a scary guy, with nearly a foot and
a hundred pounds on Alan, as well as tattoos that identified
which specific groups of people should be especially scared of
him. His daughter had met him only a handful of times, so when
her longtime and beloved foster daddy walked into the house,
she ran to him with affection and excitement. Dad did not

appreciate this and made it very clear to Alan with (let's just say) "evil" and "insult" (v. 9).

"I'm so sorry, hon," I sympathized.

A few weeks passed and Father's Day approached. "I'm going to get 'Dad' a card and frame a picture of 'kiddo' for Father's Day," I told Alan one morning.

He looked at me and took a beat. "Yep, good idea." He nodded in agreement.

It is one thing not to retaliate after an offense. It is another thing to completely forgive an offense. But it is an altogether different, irrational, supernatural, impossible-without-the-miraculous-mercy-of-God thing to *bless* after an offense.

But it is "to this you were called" (v. 9) as a disciple of Jesus. Because being repaid blessing for offense is exactly what we've received through the death of Jesus. As we were "haters of God, insolent, arrogant, boastful, inventors of evil" (Rom. 1:30 NASB), "he predestined us for adoption to himself as sons through Jesus Christ" (Eph. 1:5 ESV)—a great offense against a perfect God traded in for the very greatest of blessings from that same God.

This changes our paradigm for offense. "If you forgive others their trespasses, your heavenly Father will also forgive you, but if you do not forgive others their trespasses, neither will your Father forgive your trespasses" (Matt. 6:14–15 ESV), Jesus said, allowing us *one singular response* to the offenses of others. Being forgiven makes us into forgivers. And being extravagantly forgiven—as we've been—makes us into people who forgive *and then* pile on blessing.

Alan and I have had evil committed against us. We've been insulted. We've been accused and slandered and misjudged. And through it all, we've been convicted by God's Word to get the ultimate payback by "repay[ing] evil with blessing" (1 Pet.

3:9), not just out of obedience to God but also in trust of God. Because God promises blessing-repayers that they will "inherit a blessing" (v. 9) and ensures them that "even if [they] should suffer for what is right, [they] are blessed" (v. 14).

I've been the offender, blessed by the Offended. So when He tells me He will bless me for blessing other offenders, I believe Him.

FURTHER READING

Luke 17:1–10; 1 Peter 3

23

Be still, and know that I am God.

Psalm 46:10

I love verses that serve as a call to action to defend the vulnerable. "Speak up" (Prov. 31:8), "do justice" (Mic. 6:8 ESV), "correct oppression" (Isa. 1:17 ESV). These are the rallying cries of a heart like mine. They appeal to my sense of justice and demand action. They are a call to arms to right the wrongs of this world. These are the verses that drive me and inspire me. "Be still" (Ps. 46:10)? Not so much. I mean, I like it scrolled across lavender candles and posters of ocean scenes but not necessarily as a girding for the battle of foster parenting.

That's because the words "be still" are simply not enough on their own. In light of the injustice throughout the system and the children who need us to advocate for them, the last thing we should do is *nothing*. But being still is not about doing nothing. Being still is about actively remembering and knowing and trusting who God is.

The words "be still" aren't meant to be read and applied on their own. They simply don't work without the context of the rest of Psalm 46. They are the reaction to declarations about the God before whom we remain still.

"God is our refuge and strength, a very present help in trouble. Therefore we will not fear though the earth gives way" (v. 1). He is our protection and hiding place. He will infuse us with all the power we will need for all the things we will face. He is very present, near, and ready. So, if everything beneath me falls away, if the very ground beneath my feet disappears, I don't have to be afraid, because even then . . .

"The LORD of hosts is with us; the God of Jacob is our fortress" (v. 7). The all-powerful God who commands a battalion of angels is present and close, and the God of all history is my Protector and Keeper.

"Come behold the works of the LORD, how he has brought desolations on the earth. He makes wars cease to the end of the earth" (v. 8). So I consider and contemplate all that He's done. I remember exactly who He is and what He's capable of—commanding all of creation and all of history.

And it's then—when I know Him, when I remember what kind of God He is, when I trust His character and presence and strength—that I can be still.

This informs the way I advocate for my foster children. Foster parents are often the connecting voice between everyone involved. Many times, we understand the day-to-day needs of the kids better than anyone else, and (let's be honest) we think we know better than anyone else what's best. I'll admit, it's a struggle to advocate for my foster children from a place of stillness.

I believe that we should be speaking up, correcting oppression, and doing justice. But too often, my speaking up becomes more about convincing, any effort to correct becomes more about control, and I'm so focused on justice that I forget about trust.

"Do not be afraid," Moses said to the Israelites, who were between the proverbial rock of the approaching Egyptians and the hard place of the Red Sea. "Stand firm and you will see the deliverance the LORD will bring you today. . . . The LORD will fight for you; you need only to *be still*" (Exod. 14:13–14, emphasis mine). The people were terrified, crying out, and accusing Moses in the face of certain death. Certainly, Moses felt like this was a time for action—*Fight back, protect ourselves, do something*. But God had a plan so impossibly great (if you're not familiar with the story, let's just say, God took care of them) that it demanded stillness. Surrendered, trusting stillness allowed them to watch the Lord do what only He could do.

Foster parent: Speak up, do justice, and correct oppression. But know God's power and presence so deeply that you do it from a place of stillness.

FURTHER READING

Exodus 14; Psalm 46

24

Then the King will say to those on his right, "Come, you who are blessed by my Father; take your inheritance, the kingdom prepared for you since the creation of the world. For I was hungry and you gave me something to eat, I was thirsty and you gave me something to drink, I was a stranger and you invited me in, I needed clothes and you clothed me, I was sick and you looked after me, I was in prison and you came to visit me."

Then the righteous will answer him, "Lord, when did we see you hungry and feed you, or thirsty and give you something to drink? When did we see you a stranger and invite you in, or needing clothes and clothe you? When did we see you sick or in prison and go to visit you?"

The King will reply, "Truly I tell you, whatever you did for one of the least of these brothers and sisters of mine, you did for me."

Matthew 25:34–40

I was a stranger and you invited me in." I open the door—a toddler, terrified, unable to cry or even move. I open the door—a mother, bobbing with nervous energy and awkward excitement. I open the door—a teenager, shyly smiling, looking to please. *I invited them in.*

I've—quite literally—given food and drink to the hungry and thirsty, provided a home to the homeless, clothed the naked, nursed the sick, and visited the imprisoned as a foster parent. Foster care has invited me into serving vulnerable people in each and every way listed in this passage. And as verse 40 dramatically pulls the curtain on the eternal behind the scenes, I see that each of these small acts was so much more than an act of service to the person before me. "Truly I tell you, whatever you did for one of the least of these brothers and sisters of mine, you did for me." These are the words of the King, spoken from "his glorious throne" (v. 31) with "all the nations . . . gathered before him" (v. 32) after "the Son of Man comes in his glory" (v. 31). This is what He will say on *that* day—the one we're all living for and racing toward—when we will see Him face-to-face.

As Randy Alcorn writes, "Five minutes after we die, we'll know exactly how we should have lived. But God has given us His Word so that we don't have to wait to die to find out."* We have the five-minutes-after-death spoiler alert here: Every act of service done out of love for those in need, the vulnerable, and the hurting will be honored by the King with blessing and inheritance.

I say we live with this in view today. If everything we do for *them* is actually done for *Him*, then let's shift our mind's eye to seeing Him in all of our serving. When your kiddo with food insecurity steals food, see the face of the King. As you place the bottle into the wailing mouth of the baby for the third time in a night, see the face of the King. As you open the door to the dirty and despondent little stranger on your doorstep and welcome them home, see the face of the King. As you spend money far beyond the laughable stipend provided for clothing so you can get the perfect princess pajamas for the little princess you're caring for, see the face of the King. As you sit in the ER next to the teenager who attempted suicide, see the face of the King. As

---

*Randy Alcorn, *The Treasure Principle, Revised and Updated: Unlocking the Secret of Joyful Giving* (New York: Multnomah, 2017), 79.

you wait in a visitation room for the parent who hurt the child you love to be escorted in, orange jumpsuit and all, see the face of the King.

All of your love, all of your work, all of the giving and serving and doing is always about more than the ones you're doing it for. It's always ultimately about Him. And for all that you do for them, He will say to you, "You did it for me."

FURTHER READING

Colossians 3

25

His divine power has given us everything we need for a godly life through our
knowledge of him who called us by his
own glory and goodness.

2 Peter 1:3

L et me know if there's anything you need," the caseworker
says while I'm closing the door on her monthly check-in.
If there's anything I need? Where shall I begin? I need a
therapy referral that is less than six months from now. I need
Mom to show up for her urine screens. I need the lawyer to
respond to one of my many calls and emails. I need my kid's IEP
to be followed rather than ignored. I need the judge to hold the
caseworkers to federally mandated timelines. "We're good," I
answer with a smile.

I am well aware of all of the needs in my home and my family, and I am well aware of how the system and all the people
involved in it fall short of meeting these needs. These "needs"
can feel the most pressing. But I have a list of needs of my
own.

I need the energy to keep up with six children. I need the
supernatural power necessary to look at my child with tender-
ness as they throw the iPad down the stairs in a fit of rage. I
need to be able to fall asleep when I get in bed rather than toss
and turn in anxiety. I need wise words to advocate for my child
with strength and patience. I need an impossible kind of love
and humility to have compassion for the parent who broke her
child's leg.

I so want my foster parenting journey to be reflective of a godly life called by His own glory and goodness (2 Pet. 1:3). He is at the center—my reason, my why—to begin with. But when I'm most honest, I know that so much of it is done in my own striving self-sufficiency. I say that it's all for Him, but I forget that it's also all "from Him and through Him" (Rom. 11:36).

I worry about how I'll do all the things, without pausing to seek His direction and peace. I create my own plans and decide what's best without entrusting myself to His sovereignty. I parent my way through a tumultuous trauma meltdown without even remembering to ask His intervention. The list goes on.

This is an exhausting and disappointing way to live, trying to fulfill my needs myself when He's already provided all that I need. "[My] sufficiency is from God" (2 Cor. 3:5 ESV), and "apart from [Him I] can do nothing" (John 15:5). So why do I keep trying?

His power is divine (2 Pet. 1:3)—otherworldly, supernatural, transcendent. And it is that power that is available to me, that has *already given me* everything I need to live a godly foster parenting life. He has made Himself known to me—*I know Him*—and when I call on and cling to the knowledge I have of Him, it changes me. It meets my needs, fills in my gaps, completes my limitations.

I repent for arrogantly believing I could ever meet my own needs without Him and for being proud enough to try, and I find myself engulfed in His all-sufficient grace. "God is able to make all grace abound to you, so that *having all sufficiency in all things at all times*, you may abound in every good work" (2 Cor. 9:8 ESV). I have many needs, but "I shall not want" (Ps. 23:1 ESV).

His power provides strength and love. His power gives energy and vision. His power offers comfort and encouragement.

I want to live a godly life, but I have so many needs. And His power has given me everything I need.

FURTHER READING

Hebrews 4

26

Then Jesus told his disciples, "If anyone
would come after me, let him deny himself
and take up his cross and follow me. For whoever would save his life will lose it, but whoever loses his life for my sake will find it."

Matthew 16:24–25 ESV

I looked in the rearview mirror at my kids, their cheeks wet
and blotchy, their expressions contorted by grief. But I
didn't need to look in the mirror to know how they were
feeling; I could hear their sobs. Two and a half years is a long
time, but when you're six or seven, it's most of what you remember of your short life. We were driving their sister home, for the
final time, to be reunified with her mom, and they were feeling
their loss deeply.

When we arrived, her mom met us on the sidewalk. She saw
my forever kids and immediately burst into tears. She pulled
them all into her arms. "You listen to me," she said, forcing eye
contact with each, a guiding finger on their chins. "This is not
'goodbye'; this is 'see you soon.' She is your sister forever. We
are all a family together, forever. This is *not* 'goodbye'; this is 'see
you soon.'"

We gave our hugs and got back in the minivan, one family
member down. "She said, 'see you soon,' Mommy," my young-
est said hopefully. "When are we going to see her soon?"

"I'm not sure, baby," I answered. And we never saw her again.

"What about my kids?" is the most common—and
understandable—question I'm asked by parents considering

foster care. They want me to tell them that their children won't be hurt by foster care. They want to know that something that they choose for their kids won't be something that affects their kids. But, well, it will.

Opening your home to chaos, welcoming trauma, inviting loss can have deep and damaging effects. My kids have known pain and trauma—like the broken promise of "see you soon"—many times over. Do I make every effort to protect my kids from pain? Yes, of course I do. But do I believe that everything God allows to happen *to* them is something He is going to use *for* them? Yes, yes, even more fervently, yes. He is a God who "in all things . . . works for the good of those who love him" (Rom. 8:28), and I pray that He captures their hearts with His goodness.

I have many hopes for my children. But my greatest, most glorious hope for them is that they follow Jesus. "If anyone would come after me, let him deny himself and take up his cross and follow me" (Matt. 16:24 ESV) is the invitation of Jesus. The call to follow Jesus is a call to die. It is a happy and holy call to deny yourself and live for Christ. As foster parents, we live this dying life right before our children and invite them into the same. We show them what it is to lose our lives for His sake and find true life in Him (v. 25).

This, I believe, is the primary "lesson" of foster care for our children. They will learn so much while we walk as a family with the vulnerable—compassion, generosity, forgiveness, and love—and these are beautiful and beneficial fruits. But the bigger, broader lesson for our children is the orientation of our living as being one of dying. That rather than pursuing health and wealth and happiness, we live a life of denying and dying for Him. That just as Jesus took the burdens of the broken on His back, we follow Him as cross-carriers and love others with the same sacrificial love. And as we lose our life for His sake and find it, we discover that Jesus is truly better.

Because beyond my desire to protect my children from heartbreak and danger and difficulty, there is more I want to protect them from. I want to protect them from believing that their privileged life is to be expected or deserved rather than received with thanks as an extravagant gift from the hand of the Father (James 1:17). I want to protect them from a life that revolves around the shallow and passing pursuits of pleasure and achievement (1 John 2:17). I want to protect them from the lie that following Jesus brings ease and prosperity and demands nothing in return (Matt. 19:21; Luke 14:26). I want to protect them from being content with a life that is lived for themselves (1 Cor. 6:20).

We have a responsibility to protect our children, certainly, and to give them the best we can give them. But the very best we can give them is a glimpse of the joy of living for Jesus. So may we woo them with the surpassing worth of following Jesus and live before them the death of taking up our cross and finding life in Him.

FURTHER READING

Mark 8:34–38

27

Consider it pure joy, my brothers and sisters, whenever you face trials of many kinds, because you know that the testing of your faith produces perseverance. Let perseverance finish its work so that you may be mature and complete, not lacking anything. . . .

Blessed is the one who perseveres under trial because, having stood the test, that person will receive the crown of life that the Lord has promised to those who love him.

James 1:2–4, 12

I've never met you, but there is something I know about you for sure. You either (a) have wanted to quit foster parenting or (b) haven't been a foster parent very long. There is no third option.

I am not a quitter. I don't give up on things; I see them through. But nothing has brought me to the edge of my stick-with-it-ness like foster care.

They interrogated my children, threatened my family, opened a case against us like we were criminals. *I want to quit.*

I am punched, kicked, lied to and about, threatened. *I want to quit.*

She was in our home for two and a half years, moved to the adoption unit on the way to being a part of our forever family, and then she was sent home. *I want to quit.*

But ten years in, we haven't yet quit. We persevere.

At first mention, perseverance sounds like a wholly positive attribute. But perseverance is a quality that everyone wants and no one wants to have to acquire because there is always some level of suffering inherent to achieving it. You don't have to "persevere" tropical vacations or spa massages. Underlying the earning of perseverance is always the trial we've had to persevere.

As foster parents, we "face trials of many kinds" (v. 2)—the kinds of trials that make us want to give up, the kinds that make us feel as though we simply cannot go on. But James calls us not only to endure these trials but to "consider it pure joy" (v. 2) when we face them. Why? Because it is in them that perseverance is fought for and won.

When we "let perseverance finish its work," we are made "mature and complete, not lacking anything" (v. 4). Even better, when we persevere "under trial . . . having stood the test, [we] will receive the crown of life that the Lord has promised to those who love him" (v. 12). These are rich and eternal promises, the things that we pray for and fight for. And they are found in persevering trials.

Galatians 6 claims the just character of God as the certainty that we will reap what we sow. We are encouraged not to "become weary in doing good" because, well, it is easy to become weary in doing good. But our perseverance will be rewarded "if we do not give up" (v. 9). We can be as sure that our perseverance will be rewarded as we can be that our "God cannot be mocked" (v. 7). "We *will* reap a harvest" (v. 9, emphasis mine); we "*will* reap eternal life" (v. 8, emphasis mine).

Considering it pure joy to walk through the trials you're facing might sound like insincere make-believe. But James isn't calling us to a plastered smile or a deluded, happy-go-lucky attitude. He's calling us to see the God who is working in and above it all. Our God uses the hard things of this life to produce beautiful things in us (James 1:3), to grow us into maturity and make us complete (v. 4), to bless us with the very greatest of eternal blessings (v. 12).

So persevere, with faith and joy, trusting the God who gives us reason to—even in the midst of the trial.

FURTHER READING

James 1

28

And let us consider how to stir up one another to love and good works, not neglecting to meet together, as is the habit of some, but encouraging one another, and all the more as you see the Day drawing near.

Hebrews 10:24–25 ESV

And behold, I am with you always, to the end of the age.

Matthew 28:20 ESV

The Filled Retreat is my favorite weekend of the year. We gather one thousand foster and adoptive moms for a weekend of powerful worship, rich biblical teaching, practical workshops, and connection and laughter and fun. It is such a unique time for foster and adoptive moms, who so often feel alone and misunderstood, to feel surrounded and seen. I believe that loneliness is a common friend to foster moms who are walking through unique trials and emotions with their unique families and lifestyles. This weekend serves as a balm to the souls of many lonely foster and adoptive moms.

The pinnacle of the weekend for me—and the part that most embodies this concept of being *seen*—happens the final night each year. Each woman is given a battery-operated candle, and the lights are killed completely, leaving the room pitch black besides the one thousand artificial flames. I then walk the moms through a series of prompts and instruct them to raise their candles if the prompt applies.

"I am the mother to a child who was not born to me biologically," we begin, for practice. One thousand candles lift in solidarity and pierce the darkness. The prompts become more specific and lessen the lifted candles. "I sometimes feel as if no one in my life understands." Nine hundred candles rise. "I worry for the safety and well-being of a child who was once in my home and left." Seven hundred candles rise. "I am parenting a child who's been touched by the damaging effects of drugs and alcohol in utero." Five hundred candles rise. "I am a single mom." Three hundred candles rise. And then we finish with this hopeful declaration: "I believe that God's grace is bigger than my child's past, more powerful than my child's struggles, greater than my failures, stronger than my weaknesses, and more than enough for all that I need and all that my family needs." A thousand candles are raised together in solidarity and faith.

Audible sobs pierce the room (including those from our staff, male and female, who've watched this practice year after year), and no one is left untouched by the power of being surrounded and seen. But it's important to me that this practice is more than a passing emotional moment, which is why, beforehand, I always remind the moms of a couple of truths that they can carry with them when they return home and are no longer surrounded by one thousand women who understand. I want to remind you of the same as you sit alone in your bedroom.

First, you need community. Going to a weekend retreat is great, but you need people who are going to walk with you, people who are going to carry your burdens (Gal. 6:2), encourage you and build you up (1 Thess. 5:11), and serve you (Gal. 5:13). And people for whom—just as importantly—you are able to do the same. My hope is that you have people who understand your journey as a foster mom, speak your language, and just *get* it. But even if you don't, I hope that you lean into biblical community with people who, even if they don't understand your struggles, can walk with you in them. We are exhorted not to neglect "to meet together" because, well, it is tempting to neglect it, "as is the habit of some" (Heb. 10:25 ESV).

The model that Scripture provides for the (over one hundred) "one anothers" to be walked out is primarily in the context of the local church. For some of us, the church has not understood or surrounded our unique families in the way that it should have or been a trauma-informed, safe space for our kids. But I pray that you do not allow the failures of people to destroy your faith in His church. Find other believers; find a church family that you can do life with. You are a part of a family (Eph. 2:19), a people (1 Pet. 2:10), and a body (1 Cor. 12:12), and you simply cannot live in the fullness of the Christian life without maintaining your connection to His people.

Second, you are never alone. "I am with you always, to the very end of the age" (Matt. 28:20), Jesus encouraged His disciples and speaks to you as well. When you are afraid or overwhelmed, "It is the LORD who goes before you. He will be with you; he will not leave you or forsake you" (Deut. 31:8 ESV). When you are sorrowful, He keeps track of all your sorrows and collects all your tears in His bottle (Ps. 56:8 NLT). And when you feel just plain lonely, He "is near to all who call on him" (145:18).

"You are never any less surrounded than you are right in this moment," I remind the moms with their thousand candles lifted in solidarity and community. You, alone in your bedroom right now, are no more alone than if you were surrounded by one thousand women who understand you. God Himself is with you, and there is nothing at all like His presence.

Surround yourself with people who understand you and your journey; and if you can't find them, then people who understand your fight for faith and faithfulness. And when you're not surrounded by your people—which is eventually inevitable for all of us—remember that your God is with you always. When you feel lonely, remember that you are never alone.

FURTHER READING

Psalm 23; 1 Corinthians 12

Do not be anxious about anything, but in every situation, by prayer and petition, with thanksgiving, present your requests to God. And the peace of God, which transcends all understanding, will guard your hearts and your minds in Christ Jesus.

Philippians 4:6–7

I got a text from my current placement's worker today. "Ms. Jamie, please call me. I need to talk to you," it read. It might as well have said, "I have devastating news that will upend your life. Be afraid. Be very afraid," by the way my brain and body plummeted into anxiety.

It could have been that she'd discovered a distant second cousin in another state and they were coming to pick him up now. It could have been that there'd been an accusation and we were being investigated. It could have been that the abusive boyfriend with a frightening criminal history had been approved to live in the house with them post-reunification. Or it could have been that she needed the phone number of my babysitter. That one. It was that. She needed my babysitter's phone number.

Part of this overreaction is a learned reaction, a trauma response of sorts. You can only receive so many foster care–related, fear-inducing texts, calls, or knocks at the door before your brain flips right into fight-or-flight at the threat of one. Part of it is that as a forgetful and doubting person, I am prone to fear-filled and faithless anxiety. Part of it is that I simply don't live a lifestyle of prayer and petition, giving thanks and presenting requests to God.

This life of foster parenting is anxiety-inducing, for sure. But God commands us to "not be anxious about anything" (v. 6). "Anything" includes the rational and truly frightening things that pepper your life as they do mine. But our just and merciful God doesn't command us to do anything that His grace doesn't provide for (2 Cor. 9:8). There is a peace available to us as God's children—as foster parents—that transcends, or surpasses, all understanding. We can be filled with a peace—a divine, supernatural, God-given peace—that literally doesn't even make sense.

A distant second cousin in another state was discovered? Peace.

Accusation and investigation? Peace.

Abusive boyfriend living in the house? Peace.

Situations that should induce anxiety can be enveloped in His peace when our hearts are rooted in prayer and thanksgiving. When we trust in Him, we find that He "keep[s] him in perfect peace whose mind is stayed on [Him]" (Isa. 26:3 ESV). It's a beautiful, "vicious" cycle. We trust in Him, so we come to Him and find Him trustworthy, so we trust in Him more, and so it goes, on and on. We build the spiritual muscle memory of running to Him with petitions, requests, and gratitude and finding that His heart-and-mind-guarding peace meets us there.

The peace of God is so powerful and so pure that it can serve as a guard for our hearts and minds through truly frightening things. It is a protective force—like a burly guard or clanging gate—safely keeping what is good and defending against what is not.

Peace simply doesn't make sense in so much of what we walk through in foster care. But it's possible. Because it's a supernatural peace that is fought for and won in faithful prayer and petition and gratitude. It's a peace that's grounded in intimate relationship with and knowledge of the God who grants it. It's a peace that guards our hearts and minds in Christ Jesus.

FURTHER READING

Psalm 118

30

> Likewise the Spirit helps us in our weakness. For we do not know what to pray for as we ought, but the Spirit himself intercedes for us with groanings too deep for words. And he who searches hearts knows what is the mind of the Spirit, because the Spirit intercedes for the saints according to the will of God.
>
> Romans 8:26–27 ESV

My son is a balled-up knot of emotional contradictions. The dichotomy of the lives he's lived—in and outside of foster care—has left him heartbroken and confused about what he even wants. He desperately wants to go home. And he desperately wants to stay in our home with us. He hates the dangerous city with the dealers standing at the edge of his doorstep. And he feels restless in our slow, suburban life. He deeply loves his parents and brothers. And he feels afraid and abandoned by their dangerous and unstable way of living. He is pulled between the contradictions of both parts of his life. When I ask him how I can pray for him, it's one opposite or the other. He asks me how he should pray for himself.

And I get this. I get it in my prayers for him, for every other child I've had in my home, for their families, for myself. The simplicity of prayer is complicated by the simple fact that I often don't even know what it is I should be praying for. I know my Father is available and accessible, ready to hear and answer, but the confliction and confusion of foster care leave me unsure what to even ask.

What is right? What should happen? What is the best thing? What do I even want? I do not know what to pray for as I ought (v. 26 ESV).

Sometimes the words, and the coherent thoughts behind them, elude me completely. In times like this, I've thrown out words altogether and relied on the Spirit to communicate on my behalf. Calling His name, "Oh God, oh God, oh God," on repeat brings my heart and mind before Him in yielding worship. I don't dictate my demands or desires—I often don't even know what they are. But my wordless prayers aren't directionless; they are surrendered. "The Spirit himself intercedes for [me]," and for the times when I don't have the words, His "groanings too deep for words" are the most perfect utterances I could hope for (v. 26 ESV).

When I don't know what it is I should be praying for, I don't pray for any one thing. I simply come to my God in dependent, surrendered pleading and ask the Spirit to intercede for me. He searches my heart and knows "the mind of the Spirit" and prays only "according to the will of God" (v. 27 ESV). So there is no one better suited to pray for what I actually need than He. What a miracle that the Perfect Pray-er is praying for me on my behalf when I don't know how.

He is there to help you in your weakness. Come to Him with your fears, your hopes, your requests. And when you don't have the words to shape those, come to Him with your groans.

FURTHER READING

Ephesians 6:18–20. For more on praying for your foster children, read chapter 4 of *Foster the Family*, "I Don't Even Know How to Pray Anymore."

31

"Pardon me, my lord. As surely as you live, I am the woman who stood here beside you praying to the Lord. I prayed for this child, and the Lord has granted me what I asked of him. So now I give him to the Lord. For his whole life he will be given over to the Lord." And he worshiped the Lord there.

1 Samuel 1:26–28

The story of Hannah in just a few sentences: Hannah is one of two wives of a guy named Elkanah. She is unable to have children and is absolutely heartbroken about this. Her husband is compassionate and tender about it, but the other wife is pretty much a jerk, provoking her to the point of weeping and not eating. At the temple, Hannah—in "deep anguish" and "weeping bitterly" (v. 10)—cries out to God and basically makes a promise: If You give me a son, I'll give him right back to You. She's so distraught and unhinged that the priest, Eli, accuses her of being drunk. She explains that she is simply "deeply troubled" and in "great anguish and grief" (vv. 15, 16). Eli responds, "Go in peace, and may the God of Israel grant you what you have asked of him" (v. 17).

"The Lord remembered her" (v. 19), and Hannah gets pregnant. A couple of years later, Hannah returns to the temple and to Eli the priest and says to him, "Pardon me, my lord. As surely as you live, I am the woman who stood here beside you praying to the Lord. I prayed for this child, and the Lord has granted me what I asked of him. So now I give him to the Lord. For his whole life he will be given over to the Lord" (vv. 26–28).

This is a unique story about a unique person at a unique point in time. The direct application for foster moms in the twenty-first century is, admittedly, limited. The lesson isn't necessarily to desperately pray for a child and God will answer your prayer. And it certainly isn't to drop your three-year-old off at the local church for the pastor to raise. Yet there's something about this story that gets me, specifically, as a foster mom. There is something about the handing over of a child by a mother that makes me think of us. Something about reading of a mother entrusting her child to God that I can relate to.

Hannah received the gift of the child that she had so desperately wanted, waited for, and prayed for, but she received it differently than most mothers receive their children. She received it with hands grasped loosely around her son and a heart tightly bound to her God. She surrendered the child she so loved, not (just) into the hands of Eli but into the hands of her God. "I give him to the LORD," she says (v. 28). Or as the English Standard Version puts it, "I have lent him to the LORD."

I think that's the lesson for us. As we receive the children who are placed in our home, we receive them with a heart of surrender and faith in the God who made them, who loves them, whom they, ultimately, belong to. Our children are much safer in His hands than they are in ours, so it is a wise mother who says, "I give him to the Lord."

Immediately after Hannah surrenders her long-awaited, deeply loved, one and only son, she speaks these shocking words: "My heart rejoices in the LORD" (2:1). This reminds me of when Job loses his children (and, well, everything else) and cries, "The LORD gave, and the LORD has taken away" (Job 1:21) and blesses Him immediately after the taking. These joyful, worshipful responses are not the natural responses of parents who've lost their children. But they are the overflow of a daughter and a son so deeply rooted in submissive trust of their Father that their hearts are primed to worship Him for whatever He does. We, too, can learn to rejoice in the Lord, even as we surrender our children to Him.

"For this child I prayed; and the LORD has granted me my petition" (1 Sam. 1:27 RSV) is the echo of so many foster parents' hearts. Like Hannah, we pray, we receive, and we surrender back to Him.

FURTHER READING

1 Samuel 1–2:10

32

But do not overlook this one fact, beloved,
that with the Lord one day is as a thousand
years, and a thousand years as one day.
The Lord is not slow to fulfill his promise as
some count slowness.

2 Peter 3:8–9 ESV

My foster son is workerless, so I'm currently waiting for a new worker to be assigned. I'm waiting for this non-existent worker to do a list of other things that I've been waiting for—set up health care, establish visits, make a referral. Before this, I was waiting—for months—for a placement call, for the readiness of our family to be matched with a child who needed us. Before that, I was waiting for an adoption date for my son, waiting for the heartbreak of our last goodbye to subside, waiting for the chaos in our home to dissolve. Waiting has been a faithful—if not welcome—friend through my ten years of foster parenting.

This should be no surprise to any disciple waiting in this world. In fact, waiting is inherent to being a Christian. God's people have always been in a perpetual place of in-between—for the promised land to become home, for the Messiah to come, for the Lord to return. God's people have always been a people waiting. There has always been and will always be—until *that* day in heaven—a constant and insatiable craving for different, more, and better in the hearts of believers.

Peter reminds us not to "overlook this one fact" because he knows that we will, in fact, be very prone to overlook it: that our

God's timeline is very different from our own but that it doesn't mean He isn't doing something. As the eternal Alpha and Omega, God has a paradigm for measuring time that is different from—and much greater than—ours.

We see the here and now. Everything feels desperate and immediate, and we don't like being made to wait for what we think should happen exactly when we think it should happen.

We are like my son (biological son—no food insecurity here!). It's 4:55 p.m. and he's hungry and asks for a cereal bar. I ask him to wait just a couple more minutes, knowing that I'm putting the finishing touches on his favorite feast (homemade alfredo sauce over rigatoni with pan-fried chicken tenderloins and roasted broccoli, the favorite feast of every last one of them)—far superior to a generic strawberry cereal bar. He cries out in desperate, starving panic, "I've been waiting two hours!" He has, in fact, been waiting twenty minutes.

My child's desire for his immediate craving to be fulfilled is the most pressing thing he can see. His hunger consumes his full attention and crowds out other factors. And his understanding of time itself is so limited and immature that he can't even comprehend how short the wait has been and will be. The good I have planned is coming soon, but he doesn't grasp the timeline—or trust me—enough to wait with patience.

I think about Abraham and Sarah, who waded desperately through the pain of infertility, then waited for decades for a son to be promised and another twenty-five years for the promised son to arrive. And Genesis 21:2 oh so casually mentions, "Sarah became pregnant and bore a son to Abraham in his old age, *at the very time* God had promised him" (emphasis mine). Their waiting for a promise to be fulfilled was actually just waiting for their *desired* timeline to catch up to God's *promised* timeline.

And those timelines—and the very means for measuring the time itself—were completely different.

We understand time as children do—our immediate desires for the here and now more pressing than anything else. With our God, "one day is as a thousand years, and a thousand years as one day" (1 Pet. 3:8 ESV). He is never slow in keeping His promises; we just misunderstand slowness.

So, we wait—for workers to be assigned, for court decisions to be made, for kids to be reunified or adopted, for behaviors to change—but we are always ultimately waiting for our God to "[make] everything beautiful in its time" (Eccles. 3:11). We declare with David, "I trust in you, Lord; I say, 'You are my God.' My times are in your hands" (Ps. 31:14–15).

FURTHER READING

Matthew 5

33

"Teacher, I brought my son to you. . . . If you can do anything, have compassion on us and help us." And Jesus said to him, "'If you can'! All things are possible for one who believes." Immediately the father of the child cried out and said, "I believe; help my unbelief!" . . . Jesus took [the boy] by the hand and lifted him up, and he arose.

Mark 9:17, 22–24, 27 ESV

There's a crowd, gathered and arguing. When Jesus approaches, they "[are] greatly amazed and [run] up to him and [greet] him" (v. 15). A man emerges from the crowd with his son, who is possessed by a demon. The father is desperate for his suffering son and begs Jesus to have compassion and help "if" He can. Jesus is incensed by the man's lack of faith and exclaims, "*If?!*" The man's reaction is desperate and frantic. He immediately cries out, "I believe; help my unbelief!" (v. 24).

I know this man's "uh-oh" tone well. I hear it from my kids all the time when they react quickly, saying something they know better than to say. *Wait, wait, that's not what I meant! What I meant was . . .* The man realizes he misspoke with his "if," and he exclaims his panicked, improved reaction to the Savior: *Wait— that's not my final answer! I do believe! But I need your help because there are still the remnants of unbelief.*

I feel this so deeply. My immediate snap reaction, what spills out quickly and without thought, is the fear and faithlessness bubbling beneath the surface. Those are more convincing and more consuming. They tempt me with their pleading lies and lure me to set up my heart's camp right in the center of them. They tempt me to half-heartedly ask Jesus to help *if* He can.

Deep down in my heart, you know what I believe? I believe that God has written all the days of my family in His book and is writing a very good story for the group of us. I believe that He will accomplish His good plan in the lives of my foster children and their families. I believe that He is a God who is capable of miracles. I believe that His power has no bounds and knows no end. I believe that He always operates in His perfect love and wisdom and goodness.

But right alongside those beliefs—wrapping its strangling tendrils around my faith—is the unbelief that survives. *Foster care is ruining my family, my children. This entire case and the system are out of control. A good God would never let this happen. She's been an addict for a decade; she'll never change. If they take this child from me, it will kill me.*

What I see threatens to shrink my faith, and that is why faith is explicitly connected to "what we do not see" (Heb. 11:1)—namely, God's unseen purposes and plans and promises. In order to "walk by faith, not by sight" (2 Cor. 5:7 ESV), I have to "fix [my] eyes not on what is seen, but what is unseen" (4:18). I have to readjust my gaze past the visible and "to the King of the ages, immortal, invisible, the only God" (1 Tim. 1:17 ESV). Because what I find in Him is the source of my hope and faith for the very obvious struggles that cloud my view.

It takes a constant claim of "I believe," and a consistent confession of "help my unbelief" to hold on to faith and repent of faithlessness. It takes the supernatural, powerful help of the Savior to provide faith, which "is the gift of God" (Eph. 2:8).

Join me, friend, in bringing your children before your Savior and entrusting them to Him. Your trust may be faulty, but declare to Him that you believe Him and plead for help for your unbelief.

FURTHER READING

Hebrews 11

34

By the grace of God I am what I am.

1 Corinthians 15:10

_____

I am a good mom. I mean, I have lots of stories that display the subpar-ness of my momming, for sure. Like the time I picked up all the kids from school and drove them all over South Jersey, only to get home and realize I'd left one at day care. Or the times I dish out cereal and put on a movie and try to sell it to my kids as a fun alternative to dinner. Of course, these are the cute and shareable mom-fail stories, the kind you laugh about and put in devotionals. I also have the far-less-cute stories, the kind that I lose sleep over and weep before my God and children in repentance for. But all in all, I am a good mom.

I am a good mom because I have a great mom. My mom was (still is!) incredibly nurturing, devoted to prayer, obsessed with serving her family, endlessly joyful, consistently humble and for-giving, and all around wonderful. Between the biblical principle that when you "train up a child in the way he should go . . . he will not depart from it" (Prov. 22:6 ESV) and the healthy attach-ment model handed me by my mom on a golden platter, I had a leg up in this whole motherhood thing. *By the grace of God I am what I am.*

And for the times that, well, I'm not a great mom, for the I-forgot-to-pick-up-my-kid-at-day-care days, I have a support sys-tem that shows up for me. My husband and family and friends, my bank account and education, my community and church all surround me as a safety net that is impossible to adequately valuate—until I imagine life without it. I didn't do anything to deserve these people, this help, this life. *By the grace of God I am what I am.*

When I compare my reality—what I experienced as a child and experience still today—to the reality of most of the moms of most of the kids I've cared for, I can't help but be struck with the chasm of disparity in our stories.

All that I have and all that I am is simply and solely a "good and perfect gift . . . from above, coming down from the Father" (James 1:17). None of it was earned, none of it was deserved, none of it came because of my goodness or superiority. It is all only a gift, beginning first with my salvation and adoption. And the more I am aware of God's extraordinary, undeserved gifts to me, the more my heart soars in gratitude to Him and bends in humility toward others.

"What do you have that you did not receive? If then you received it, why do you boast as if you did not receive it" (1 Cor. 4:7 ESV). Paul pierces my heart in interrogation. My questions of *How could you . . . ? Why don't you . . . ? How come you . . . ?* directed toward my kids' parents melt away before this reproach.

As my awareness of my own weakness, sin, and indebtedness to God and others grows, my humility increases (see Eph. 2:8–9). My compassion multiplies. My understanding that nothing I've become or overcome really has anything at all to do with me. I learn "not to think of [myself] more highly than [I] ought to think, but to think with sober judgment" (Rom. 12:3 ESV).

To whom much is given, much is required (Luke 12:48), and I have been given so much. I pray that I become more aware of all that's been given, so that it may overflow into gratitude to God and humility toward my kids' parents.

Note: Maybe your story mirrors mine—a happy and healthy childhood, a loving and supportive network. Or maybe it's more similar to your kids' parents'—struggle and scarcity and lack of safety. No matter the case, God's grace in your life remains. If you've had the strength and resilience, the support and resources, the miraculous grace to overcome it all, then you, too, can say, "By the grace of God I am what I am" (1 Cor. 15:10), and be overwhelmed with gratitude and humility.

FURTHER READING

Ephesians 2

35

Every good and perfect gift is from above, coming down from the Father of the heavenly lights, who does not change like shifting shadows. He chose to give us birth through the word of truth, that we might be a kind of firstfruits of all he created.

James 1:17–18

I took my teenage (biological) daughter to her favorite store, and together we filled a cart—a fun journal and some pens, hair clips, lip balm, fuzzy socks, gum, a reusable water bottle, the kinds of things that teenage girls go crazy for. But the cartful of goodies wasn't for her. Another teenage girl would be joining our family the next day, and we wanted her to have something right away to call her own and—on a sad and scary day—hopefully make her smile.

The next day she walked through the door of her new bedroom with every single thing she owned in her hands. "This is a little something for you," I said nonchalantly as I pointed to the basket.

She smiled shyly. "Thank you."

When she came downstairs later wearing, holding, or using nearly everything in the basket—hair clipped back, shiny lips, and fuzzy socks on as she chewed gum, held her journal tightly, and filled up her water bottle—she thanked me again.

"Of course, honey. That was just some fun stuff so you can have some things that are just yours. We'll go to the store together tomorrow to get you any clothes you need."

She looked at her hands for a minute. "My last foster home took the clothing check to Walmart and brought me back three identical T-shirts and sweatpants in different colors. When I asked her if I could pick out my own clothes, she said that I was being ungrateful. They're still in the Walmart bag in my suitcase upstairs."

"That sucks," I answered. "You should get to pick out your own clothes. That's how we do things here."

I'd known this girl for a few hours, but before I even met her, my heart was aching: *I want her to feel at home. I want to make her smile. I want her to feel loved.* My mother's heart for her wasn't dependent on what kind of kid she would be; it was driven by the maternal claim of "now my own" that is inherent to motherhood. I wanted to give this girl good gifts.

Jesus draws the analogy between our parental desire to bless our children with good things and His (superior) generosity as a frame of reference for understanding the Father's heart. "Which of you," He asks, "if your son asks for bread, will give him a stone? Or if he asks for a fish, will give him a snake? If you, then, though you are evil, know how to give good gifts to your children, how much more will your Father in heaven give good gifts to those who ask him!" (Matt. 7:9–11).

My (foster) mother love pales in comparison to the great love of the Father. I want to bless and provide and give good gifts, and I do. But the gifts I give are limited and incomplete. They never fully satisfy and don't ever last, and—because they come from "evil" me (v. 11)—they're tainted by selfishness and touched by sin.

But the gifts He gives me as His daughter? They are good. They are perfect. They come down from Him above, and they rest on His unchanging nature. Like a daughter asking a generous father for bread, I can approach with humble expectation that He will feed and satisfy.

My confidence in His blessings is rooted in the truth that He "chose to give [me life] through the word of truth" (James 1:18), His Son, Jesus. I know God is a Good-Gift Giver because I have been the recipient of the very best gift. Salvation, redemption, adoption, everlasting life are mine in Him. As I receive other wonderful—but ultimately lesser—gifts, I am drawn to wonder and worship of His generosity. I know what it is to be a mother wanting to bless her children, and I am, well, evil.

But He is the God who gives good and perfect gifts, and as His daughter, I am the grateful recipient.

FURTHER READING

Psalm 84

36

Vindicate me, O LORD,
>for I have walked in my integrity,
>and I have trusted in the LORD without
>wavering.

Psalm 26:1 ESV

The worker's name was Jamie. I remember that, for obvious reasons. And I remember how it felt. Like shame, like rage, like terror. The accusation was bogus, but it didn't matter. I was being accused, and a worker—the same kind of worker who removed other kids from other homes and brought them to mine—was interrogating and investigating *me*.

When she left, I went into fix-it mode. Don't they know that I'm a leader in the foster care community? Well, I'm going to parlay any sort of status I can. I called the highest person in the county—direct line, first-name basis. I told her what had happened. I told her it was bogus. As my voice and hands shook, I took control of the situation. And she all but hung up on me. I felt completely powerless as I internally scrambled for the next step and was left wanting. I had no recourse, no big idea. There was literally nothing for me to do.

I reached out to friends in a panic, and one sent back four words—the words of Psalm 26:1—that were an immediate salve to my soul. "Vindicate me, O LORD," became more than a meditation for me. It became a mantra. A fearful thought, an angry feeling, a desperate idea would fire up, and I would douse it right back down again with this prayer.

"What if they take my kids from me?" *Vindicate me, O LORD.*

"What kind of monster would make this accusation?" *Vindi-cate me, O LORD.*

"What if I just call this person and convince them to . . . ?" *Vindicate me, O LORD.*

The psalmist knew unjust accusations. David was hated and pursued and conspired against—by the king. David's prayer in Psalm 26:1—as well as the rest of the chapter—serves as a prayer of desperation that we can borrow in our own experience of unjust accusation.

David cries out for his God to vindicate him because he has done the right thing ("for I have walked in my integrity") and trusts the Lord ("I have trusted in the LORD without wavering"). He prays faith-filled prayers for vindication because he knows that he was not in the wrong and that his God is trustworthy.

Foster long enough, and you will encounter misunderstandings and unjust accusations, if not outright interrogations and investigations. Few things will rob your sense of control like being misunderstood, misjudged, and threatened. Do you believe that God can vindicate you? Even better than you can vindicate yourself? Then ask Him to. And then ask Him again and again.

When there's nothing more that you can do, keep walking in your integrity, keep doing what is right, and trust that your Lord will take care of you. David ends Psalm 26 where he began: "But as for me, I shall walk in my integrity; redeem me, and be gracious to me" (v. 11 ESV). His big plan? Keep doing what's right and trust his God to be the One to vindicate him.

FURTHER READING

Psalm 26

37

Trust in the LORD with all your heart
    and do not lean on your own
        understanding.
In all your ways acknowledge him,
    and he will make straight your paths.

Proverbs 3:5–6 ESV

I've been a foster parent for over ten years. I've spent seven years supporting foster parents and training and teaching about foster care. I've read research, learned interventions, and studied policy. I've gathered a good amount of "understanding" surrounding all things foster care.

Left to my own devices, I lean hard on that understanding. When a caseworker tries to enforce something that is incorrect or simply preference, I (kindly) cite policy, reach out to their supervisor, and follow up with an email cc'ing all the people about how an accurate application of policy should function. When my child is having a trauma response, I recall my TBRI (Trust-Based Relational Intervention) training, I pull out my trusty scripts, and I access my child's "toolbox." (Cue self-satisfied pat on the back.)

Learning is an important part of this foster care journey. I would encourage every foster parent to learn—about policy and trauma and attachment and all things foster care. But as your understanding grows, so can the temptation to depend on—lean on—your own understanding. Knowledge and understanding can make it harder to sit back, surrender, and *trust*.

I often believe I know what is best—for my family, my kids, their case. Maybe sometimes I do. But more often, I am being led by my own pride. I don't simply hold information or insight; I believe I have *understanding*, that I have *the* answer. Proverbs warns against people like me. "Do you see a man who is wise in his own eyes? There is more hope for a fool than for him" (26:12 ESV). Paul commands directly, "Never be wise in your own sight" (Rom. 12:16 ESV).

A humble woman surrenders her knowledge before His. "Have you not known? Have you not heard?" Isaiah questions us. "The LORD is the everlasting God, the Creator of the ends of the earth . . . his understanding is unsearchable" (40:28 ESV). "Oh, the depth of the riches and wisdom and knowledge of God!" Paul reminds us. "How unsearchable are his judgments and how inscrutable his ways!" (Rom. 11:33 ESV).

Our knowledge is incomplete, insufficient, faulty, and touched by our sin. His knowledge is unsearchable, deep, rich, inscrutable. It's not only that we *should not* trust in *our* own knowledge, out of humble obedience. It's that we are *invited to* trust in *His* superior knowledge, in faith that it is actually better. We are told not to lean on our own understanding because trusting Him is a far better proposition.

More than knowledge, I want wisdom. And wisdom does not come from gaining more information; it comes from Him. "If any of you lacks wisdom, let him ask God, who gives generously to all without reproach, and it will be given him" (James 1:5 ESV). My understanding, without wisdom and humility, is useless, but "with the humble is wisdom" (Prov. 11:2 ESV).

As I walk with my children on the path of foster care— through the system, through trauma, through all that we face—I want to lean on something more stable than my faulty and failing understanding. His absolute knowledge and perfect wisdom are available, and all I have to do is trust Him, acknowledge Him, and rely on Him. And as I surrender all that I know to Him in faith, He will be the One to make the path straight.

FURTHER READING

Proverbs 3

38

Into your hands I commit my spirit.

Psalm 31:5 and Luke 23:46

'm reading 1 Samuel right now in my daily devotions. David defeats Goliath and becomes the new man of the hour, garnering the praise of the people and gaining the favor of King Saul. That is, until he loses said favor. Saul goes out of his mind (maybe even demon possessed?) and takes to pretty regularly throwing spears at David and trying to kill him, so David goes on the lam.

Psalm 31 was written while David was in hiding, his life being threatened by the murderous king. He cries,

> Be merciful to me, LORD, for I am in distress;
>   my eyes grow weak with sorrow,
>   my soul and body with grief.
> My life is consumed by anguish
>   and my years by groaning;
>   my strength fails because of my affliction,
>   and my bones grow weak. (vv. 9–10)

David is my guy. Because he doesn't mince words. He doesn't sugarcoat anything. He lays it out, authentic and raw and exactly as it is.

The sorrow, the grief, the anguish and groaning and failing strength are something I can very much relate to. When my foster daughter left my home after two and a half years, those were the words I would've used. Groaning and grieving, lying in bed with teary eyes, shoveling bread into my mouth. If I would've written a psalm, it would've echoed the tone of Psalm 31.

I don't know what your sorrowful, grief-filled, anguished and groaning and strength-failing moments are, but I know you've had them. As a foster parent, you've most likely had many of them. And in these moments, what else can you do except cry out to your loving Lord, "Into your hands I commit my spirit" (v. 5)? I have echoed these words with both desperation and faith behind them. And in echoing them, I am in very good company.

Luke 23 sets the scene dramatically: "It was now about noon, and darkness came over the whole land until three in the afternoon, for the sun stopped shining. And the curtain of the temple was torn in two" (vv. 44–45). And then, echoing the words He had ordained for David to scrawl about a thousand years before, "Jesus called out with a loud voice, 'Father, into your hands I commit my spirit.' When he had said this, he breathed his last" (v. 46).

As David experienced loss, suffering, betrayal, and fear, he committed his spirit into the hands of the Lord. He entrusted himself into the loving and sovereign care of his Father, because he believed that he would "look upon the goodness of the Lord in the land of the living" (Ps. 27:13 ESV). *How much more* can we, who have the ultimate proof of the love and sovereignty of God in the finished work of Christ, entrust ourselves into His hands? David was waiting in faith for the Messiah he believed would eventually come; we get to rest in peace in the Messiah who's *already* come.

Jesus's cry of "into your hands I commit my spirit" is the very reason we can cry out, with absolute confidence, "into your hands I commit my spirit." Jesus's death on the cross purchased for us the hope that through our sorrow, grief, anguish, groaning, and failing strength, His love for us is a trustworthy, deserving-of-committing-our-spirit-into kind of love.

FURTHER READING

Luke 23

39

Beloved, let us love one another, for love is from God, and whoever loves has been born of God and knows God. Anyone who does not love does not know God, because God is love. In this the love of God was made manifest among us, that God sent his only Son into the world, so that we might live through him. In this is love, not that we have loved God but that he loved us and sent his Son to be the propitiation for our sins. Beloved, if God so loved us, we also ought to love one another. No one has ever seen God; if we love one another, God abides in us and his love is perfected in us. . . .

We love because he first loved us.

1 John 4:7–12, 19 ESV

"Good night, girls. I love you," I say as I pull the door closed to my teenage daughters' room. I hear the singular "I love you too" that I expect back from my oldest, biological daughter, but then I hear a second "I love you too." This one I didn't expect; this one from the teenager who joined our family about a month before. Once she said it, she couldn't stop saying it. It was like the floodgates burst and she didn't want to hold it in anymore. I told her I loved her dozens of times a day, often in response to her saying the three words first.

Love is about as central to the job of mothering—in all motherhood, including and especially foster motherhood—as a thing can be. But not necessarily in the way we typically think of it.

Somehow, somewhere, *love* became defined as a feeling rather than an action. The words we use to describe love—like that love is something that overcomes you, something you fall into—certainly don't help. Love is not a passive feeling that happens to you; love is something you put on, something you choose, something you do. As the OG nineties Christian rap group DC Talk famously rhymed, love is a verb.

First John 4:7 calls and commands us to "love one another" using the Greek verb for love, *agape*, a form of love that the *Cambridge Dictionary* calls "a giving love, entirely unselfish."* John tells us, as the followers of Jesus, to *do* love by giving to someone else and giving to them at our own expense.

This definition of love, of course, checks out with the next verse that tells us that "God is love" because this is exactly what God has done for us. "The love of God was made manifest among us" when "God sent his only Son into the world" (v. 9 ESV). Jesus—God Himself, Love Itself—was made manifest, came to earth, and showed us what love looks like walking around with skin on. And what it looks like: death. It looks like dying for those you love. "Greater love has no one than this, that someone lay down his life for his friends" (John 15:13 ESV).

This is the kind of love we're called to as foster moms—not a feely, falling-into kind of love but a doing, dying kind of love. The good news is that as we are commanded to *give* this kind of love, we are reminded that we are first the *recipients* of this kind of love. "We love because he first loved us" (1 John 4:19) doesn't mean primarily that we *should* love with a doing, dying kind of love because of how we've been loved. It means that we *can* love with a doing, dying kind of love because of how we've

---

Cambridge Dictionary, s.v. "agape (n.)," accessed July 31, 2023, https://dictionary.cambridge.org/us/dictionary/english/agape.

been loved. It's less of a prescription and more of a diagnosis. *Because* God loved us first, we are now able to love others.

The key to it all is in the very first verse of this passage, "Beloved, let us love . . ." (v. 7 ESV). We skip right along to the "to do," but the command to *do* something is first preceded by the reminder that we *are* something: beloved. Our call to remember our identity as beloved by God precedes and motivates and—best of all—empowers the call to love anyone else.

FURTHER READING

1 John 4

40

We do not know what to do, but our eyes are on you.

2 Chronicles 20:12

Every day, dozens of times a day, I get questions on Instagram from people looking for direction for their foster parenting journey. "I've learned so much from you," or "I really respect your opinion," they all begin. And then they end with a question that essentially equates to *What should I do?*: "Is this having a negative impact on my forever children?" "I don't feel like I can do this anymore; should I disrupt?" "Should I call CPS on bio Mom after what I just discovered?" "What should I do?"

It's an honor to be invited into people's lives and journeys like this. I don't resent the questions, but most often I want to answer, "I have no idea what to do in my own life; I can't begin to tell you what to do in yours."

I have my own questions about my own family that I wish I could bring to someone else for a concise and perfect answer. *Should we move forward with adopting this child? Should we try a different, much more serious medication? Should we switch schools? Should I reach out to Mom again after losing contact? What should I do?*

Very few of the challenging questions we face as foster parents have a right or wrong answer. It's very rarely an issue of choosing the clearly correct option and usually an issue of pursuing wisdom.

All throughout Proverbs are rich descriptions of the benefits of wisdom. Proverbs 3 declares, "Blessed are those who find wisdom, those who gain understanding" (v. 13), then goes on to describe wisdom as more precious and valuable than silver, gold, and rubies (vv. 14–15) and charges, "Do not let wisdom and understanding out of your sight, preserve sound judgment and discretion; they will be life for you" (vv. 21–22).

If wisdom is so valuable, then how can we acquire it? Most simply put: by seeking God. We read in Proverbs 9:10 that "the fear of the LORD is the beginning of wisdom," and while the fear of the Lord is not easily defined, one way to understand it is abbreviated by John Piper with this sentence: "Fearing God means that God is, in your mind and heart, so powerful and so holy and so awesome that you would not dare to run away from him, but only run to him."*

Fearing God and finding wisdom start with seeking God. We seek and find Him—and wisdom—when we study His character and commands in Scripture. We seek and find Him—and wisdom—when we come to Him in prayer and petition. We seek and find Him—and wisdom—when we gather with His people and sit under the preaching of His Word.

I have no problem with anyone asking me for my advice—I go to others myself—but my question to them and to my own heart is this: Did you go to God first? How often do we seek wisdom in people, opinions, books, and experts and neglect the very Source of wisdom Himself? "If any of you lacks wisdom, let him ask God, who gives generously to all without reproach, and it will be given him," says James 1:5 (ESV). Maybe you will pray and "your ears will hear a voice behind you, saying, 'This is the way; walk in it'" (Isa. 30:21). Most likely, you won't. When Chris-

---

*John Piper, "Flee to Christ in Fear," Desiring God, accessed July 31, 2023, https://www.desiringgod.org/interviews/flee-to-christ-in-fear?fbclid=IwAR3R cyu_9TNAjn_gOjvfs_cR4mVXiJAhuwAwzHy9kwQr6MANm3sPmbCVOK4.

tians talk about hearing God, they rarely mean audibly listening to a voice and usually mean some combination of experiencing a guiding thought in prayer, reading or remembering something instructive in God's Word, having another believer share something helpful, or feeling an overwhelming sense of peace or direction. Don't discredit this. "The LORD will guide you always" (58:11), and He will use His Word, His people, and His presence to do so.

As you wrestle through the uncertainties of foster care and wish you could bring the hard questions to God Himself, don't forget that Jesus told His disciples that it was to their advantage that He go away so that He could send the Helper to them (John 16:7). The Holy Spirit is called our Helper, and He is not only *with* us, He is *in* us (1 Cor. 3:16). When we feel confused and uncertain, may we find great comfort in the constant indwelling of God Himself in us through the Holy Spirit. While it would be great to have God walking by our side, it is even better to have Him *within* us.

Remember that "the LORD gives wisdom" (Prov. 2:6), and as you seek wisdom, seek Him "in whom are hidden all the treasures of wisdom" (Col. 2:3).

FURTHER READING

Proverbs 2

41

Come with me . . . to a quiet place and get some rest.

Mark 6:31

There was violent banging and screaming—hysterics—downstairs. I shot up in bed, my heart pounding so intensely I could feel it in my ears. I was overcome with panic, my breath became short and labored, and the room started spinning. That's when I realized the hysterics were laughing, the banging was dancing, and the screaming was singing. It was my kids having fun together.

I've had similar over-the-top reactions to just as benign scenarios. A loud banging at the door (CPS investigation?), a late-night call from Mom (she relapsed?), an unexpected meeting with the principal (they're kicking her out of school?) can raise my blood pressure in a moment. Maybe I sound like a worrywart, but I promise you I'm not—or at least, I never used to be. Every scenario I've listed is one I've experienced before—a sound, a call, a moment that completely changes our lives and tailspins our family into chaos. These are not irrational overreactions. They are learned trauma responses to traumatic scenarios. My brain and body have been primed by the chaos of foster care to be ready for every last thing and react with appropriate survival instincts.

This means that combating my newfound anxiety is about more than just believing truth in my heart; it's about pursuing rest for my body. Secondary trauma (the trauma we incur from caring for the traumatized) and primary trauma (the trauma we incur from chronic stress, loss, the system, and traumatizing behaviors) are a risk for every foster parent. And as physical and spiritual beings, the solution is both physical and spiritual. In this case, we see modern psychology and biblical wisdom work in concert neatly. We've talked all throughout this book about believing gospel truths; now it's time to talk about believing and applying what God says about the physical needs of our bodies too.

God created our bodies with inherent needs, needs that too often we attempt to overcome, to "hack," to get by without having to take the time to fulfill. But these needs are *from* God so that they can be filled *by* God and keep us dependent *on* God. It is all a part of our acknowledging and remembering that we are not self-sustaining or self-sufficient but completely reliant on Him. Part of claiming that "when I am weak, then I am strong" (2 Cor. 12:10) is humbly coming to Him in our weakness—not charging forward as though we're not weak—so that we can find strength and rest for our hearts, brains, and bodies.

Your body needs sleep and sunlight, food and water, laughter and touch, and the source of each of these things is outside of yourself. "In him we live and move and exist" (Acts 17:28 NLT). Surrendering to these needs is inherently humbling; they are important reminders that we are created beings.

When we consider "WWJD," the Gospels provide a compelling example. "Jesus often withdrew to lonely places and prayed" (Luke 5:16). We see Him taking naps (Mark 4:38), "[withdrawing] by boat privately to a solitary place" (Matt. 14:13), and entering a house and not wanting anyone to know it (Mark 7:24). Jesus was God and could've divinely downloaded the strength and rest He needed, but He modeled for us a life of mission that was intentionally recharged and called His followers to the same. When His disciples were run ragged "because so many people were coming and going that they did not even have a chance to eat, he said to them, 'Come with me by yourselves to a quiet place and get some rest'" (6:31). This is the Savior's example, these are the Savior's words, this is the Savior's heart for you.

Are you honoring the rhythms of input and output that God placed within your body? Are you experiencing—or at least pursuing—seven hours of sleep, some physical activity, eight glasses of water, healthy meals, laughter and friendship, and regular times of prayer and Bible reading? If not, why not? There are seasons when these things are not possible, but if you find (like I've been guilty of myself) that a season becomes a lifestyle, then you might need to ask deeper, harder questions, like *How might my too-busy lifestyle actually be evidence of pride? Do I believe God will fill in gaps in my life and family that slowing down might reveal? Am I resisting God's invitation and command to rest? Do I trust God enough to rest?*

God wants to meet you in your exhaustion, in your weakness, in your stress. He invites you to take care of the body that He created and called good, to humbly submit to how He made you to be, to come with Him to a quiet place and get some rest.

FURTHER READING

Acts 17:25; Psalm 16

42

All the days ordained for me were written
   in your book
before one of them came to be.

Psalm 139:16

The very first child to enter my home through foster care eventually became my forever child through adoption. Similar to all the "firsts" I experienced with my first biological daughter, all my foster parenting "firsts" were experienced with her. She was the first child dropped off at my doorstep who, in a moment, went from stranger to daughter. She was the first child I parented who had experienced trauma and introduced me to the confusing paradigm of a young brain left wanting by what she hadn't received. She was the first of my children who experienced the loss of her parents and the finality of the legal loss of them through termination.

I was overwhelmed with the awareness of her story—her two and a half years in foster care, the year of her life before she came to our family, her nine months in the womb, the twenty-five years her mother lived before having her—and so on. Her story didn't begin when she showed up on our doorstep. There were many characters and plotlines that preceded us, and they remained tethered still.

When it came time to adopt her and make her a Finn, we were choosing her middle name, and I knew exactly what it should be: Story. This little girl's life was not simply and only the result of other people's decisions and actions; it was a story written by the Author of her life.

Throughout the Old and New Testaments, God's sovereignty in accomplishing His purposes—unfolding the story He's written—is on display. He speaks through Isaiah:

> I am God, and there is no other;
>> I am God, and there is none like me.
> I make known the end from the beginning,
>> from ancient times, what is still to come.
> I say, "My purpose will stand,
>> and I will do all that I please." (46:9–10)

He alone is the Author of the story He's composed.

Though we are living in the messy middle of a story still unfolding, we can cling to a very good ending because that ending has already been "predestined according to the plan of him who works out everything in conformity with the purpose of his will" (Eph. 1:11). Paul tells us that "we know that in all things God works for the good of those who love him, who have been called according to his purpose. For those God foreknew he also predestined to be conformed to the image of his Son. . . . And those he predestined, he also called; those he called, he also justified; those he justified, he also glorified" (Rom. 8:28–30). I assure you that I am not yet, in fact, "glorified," but His already-written purpose is so certain that it's as though it's already complete. We can know, with surety, that it's all going to work out for good because God has already written the final pages of the complete story of humanity. These words are certain and should bolster us in the uncertainty of this life.

Of course, the most beautiful words authored about our lives are that our "names are written in heaven" (Luke 10:20), recorded in "the Lamb's book of life" (Rev. 13:8). Our names, scrawled in the inerasable blood of Jesus, are certainly, for each of us, the single greatest word written on any page of any book.

Life can feel chaotic and out of control. It's easy for me to point to judges and workers as the ones determining my fate. It's easy for me to watch the decisions of others and elevate them above God's sovereign control. But life is not random, none of it is accidental, none of it is actually determined by anyone else. It is all lovingly authored by my God in heaven.

As we consider our children's stories—and I know how broken and heartbreaking some of them can be—our confidence is not in the hope of a happily ever after. Our confidence is in knowing the Author. When we look at the pages that have passed and we're filled with confusion or fear for the future, "let us fix our eyes on Jesus, the author and perfecter of our faith" (Heb. 12:2 BSB).

FURTHER READING

Ephesians 1

43

You have not spoken the truth about me, as my servant Job has.

Job 42:7

I pressed the "follow" button reluctantly. This wasn't a page for me. These posts were for people in grief, people who'd had someone they loved die. But I couldn't stop reading and crying. Maybe this account wasn't for me, but its message was—it resonated and relieved with its raw reflections on loss.

I used to think of grieving as something you did when someone you loved died, but over my ten years of foster parenting, my understanding of grief has broadened quite a bit to include many different kinds of losses and sorrows, including my own.

Loss is inherent to foster parenting, as it is to any sort of role or relationship that is temporary. I have said goodbye to over twenty-five foster children. Some of them left me with pangs of sadness, some with deep wounds of sorrow, but each left their mark. It doesn't matter that I pray for it and work toward it; when it happens, I grieve it.

This is an obvious grief, but there's another kind of grief I've experienced as a foster parent that has nothing to do with saying goodbye to a child. It's the loss of "normal," the loss of how things were "supposed" to be, the loss of expectations. I "expected" to be able to leave our kids with babysitters for regular date nights. I thought kids were "supposed" to enjoy fun, spontaneous family nights. "Normal" families aren't investigated by CPS. I carry the loss of the way things were or were never able to be.

Job was "blameless and upright" (1:1), a man whom God regarded as a trophy of faithful servanthood. Very long story, very shortly told, God allows Satan to afflict Job with every kind of grief—because He wants to reveal Himself to Job (and to the rest of us who get to follow along). In Job 1 and 2, Job loses everything—all his children, all his wealth, and his health. The next forty-one chapters walk us through how he wrestles with God through his grief.

Most of the book of Job is dialogue between Job and his friends—that is, until God comes on the scene and interrupts their blathering with His faith-producing rebuke. Job does a lot of the talking, and he is, to say the least, conflicted—fluctuating from questioning his own heart ("Shall we receive good from God, and shall we not receive evil?" [2:10 ESV]) to expressing desperation ("I loathe my life; I would not live forever" [7:16 ESV]). He swings from challenging God to worshiping God, asking, "Why do you hide your face and count me as your enemy?" (13:24 ESV) before confidently declaring, "I know that my Redeemer lives" (19:25 ESV). Job has many conflicted and confusing thoughts and questions and emotions, but he brings them all before God.

My favorite words and the lesson for us come at the end of the book, after Job and his friends do a whole lot of talking: "You have not spoken the truth about me, *as my servant Job has*" (42:7, emphasis mine), God says in rebuke of Job's friends and commendation of Job. These words are shocking, as some of the words Job spoke about God were not actually true. He had not spoken only completely true things about God, but God approved of his words because they were ultimately spoken in fear of Him.

Job's words—as messy and mistaken as they may have been—were faith-filled and worshipful because they were directed *to* God in *faith* rather than *at* God in *accusation*. As Job wrestled with his losses, he brought his questions and his sorrow before his God. He didn't, ultimately, "grieve as others do who have no hope" (1 Thess. 4:13 ESV). He engaged with God until he encountered Him and the hope He brings. It was in the midst of his grief that he declared, "The LORD gave, and the LORD has taken away; *blessed be the name of the LORD*" (Job 1:20–21 ESV, emphasis mine).

We, too, can grieve in a holy and honest way—acknowledging our deep sorrow, bringing our questions to God, struggling toward Him, surrendering to Him. What better place to bring our grief than to the One who "has borne our griefs" (Isa. 53:4 ESV)? What better way to walk through our sorrows than to run to the One who "carried our sorrows" (v. 4 ESV)? He can handle your wondering and your wavering, and He wants to meet you in the middle of it. So, like Job, come with faith—as beat up and broken as it may be—and "in all this . . . [do] not sin or charge God with wrong" (1:22 ESV).

FURTHER READING

Job 38–40

44

Take every thought captive to obey Christ.

2 Corinthians 10:5 ESV

She's going to wake up in the middle of the night and she's not going to know where she is. She's going to be stuck in a strange bed in a strange room in a strange house. She's going to cry out for Mommy, and I won't be there to answer. She's not going to understand. She's going to think I abandoned her.

The thoughts crashed over me like violent ocean waves of nausea, fear, guilt, and hopelessness, the strength of their tide pulling me under, taking my breath away. It was my daughter's first overnight visit with her mom. She began crying as soon as she recognized the neighborhood from the window. How could I explain to her that I didn't want to leave her? How could I let her know that I would come back? Worst of all: How would I help her understand what was happening the final time, the time that I wouldn't be coming back? I lay in bed awake and worrying the whole night through.

We talk a lot about our emotions in foster care—getting "too attached," having a broken heart—but I am convinced that it's not our hearts that get us into trouble; it's our minds.

"Take every thought captive to obey Christ," Paul exhorts the Corinthians (2 Cor. 10:5 ESV). The underlying subtext of this command: Your thoughts are not going to stay where they should. They're going to go awry, veer off track, get you in trouble. And "the power of positive thinking" won't be enough. You'll need the ferocity of captivity to keep them obedient.

Paul encourages the Philippians to think about "whatever is true, whatever is honorable, whatever is just, whatever is pure, whatever is lovely, whatever is commendable, if there is any excellence, if there is anything worthy of praise" (Phil. 4:8 ESV). This may seem delusional as a foster parent, but this isn't about playing pretend. This is about making our thinking obedient to Christ. We don't attempt to simply will ourselves out of negative thinking. We rely on the Spirit, the Helper, to bring to our remembrance all that Jesus has said (John 14:26 ESV). We remember gospel truths that can captivate our thoughts into obedience.

We comfort our anxious thoughts with the reminder that God promises, "I am with you . . . I am your God; I will strengthen you, I will help you, I will uphold you with my righteous right hand" (Isa. 41:10 ESV). We chastise our judgmental thoughts with the reminder that we condemn ourselves when we judge others (Rom. 2:1) and that "God opposes the proud but gives grace to the humble" (James 4:6 ESV). We tame the imaginative plans that we're willing for our future with the reminder that "the heart of man plans his way, but the LORD establishes his steps" (Prov. 16:9 ESV).

On the cross, Jesus purchased our peace. "Peace with God" (Rom. 5:1), first and foremost. But also, experiential peace that can be ours while we walk through the unpeaceful parts of this life. "Peace I leave with you;" He said to His disciples, "my peace I give to you . . . let not your hearts be troubled, neither let them be afraid" (John 14:27 ESV). His peace—which He's already given to us—can guard us from fear.

Your mind is the battlefield of foster care, and it's here that you must wage war and take captives. It produces thoughts and narratives and beliefs that shape your emotions, your decisions, your actions, and your relationships. So, "let the peace of Christ rule in your hearts" (Col. 3:15).

FURTHER READING

Philippians 4

45

The angel of the LORD found Hagar near a spring in the desert. . . .

She gave this name to the LORD who spoke to her: "You are the God who sees me," for she said, "I have now seen the One who sees me."

Genesis 16:7, 13

Meet Hagar. Hagar is a woman enslaved, handmaiden to Sarai.

Sarai is better known as Sarah, as in Abraham and Sarah, whom God makes a covenant with—in the midst of decades of infertility—that they will not only have a son but that their children will outnumber the very stars themselves. They question and laugh over this promise because, well, they're very, very old. Sarai doubts God's plan and gets impatient and decides to take matters into her own hands. "Go, sleep with my slave; perhaps I can build a family through her" (v. 2), she says to Abram (later to become Abraham), which is a pretty shaky plan from the outset and turns out exactly as you might expect it would. Hagar becomes pregnant and despises Sarai (understandably so, as she's the woman who handed Hagar over to her husband to be raped). This woman—whose body doesn't legally or functionally belong to herself, who has no rights to say yes or no, who was given by the wife to be raped by the husband, becomes, again, the victim of this couple. Sarah mistreats the woman she subjected to this abuse and Abraham just lets it happen. Completely desperate, Hagar runs away into the desolate and threatening desert.

It is in this nothingness—with no rights, no one to provide for her or protect her, no family, no support system, no one at all—that she is visited by the Lord Himself. He questions her, He directs her, and then He speaks about her son's destiny. Finally, Hagar responds and "she gave this name to the LORD who spoke to her: 'You are the God who sees me,' for she said, 'I have now seen the One who sees me'" (v. 13).

Up to this point, no one—male, female, important, faithful, free, or enslaved—has given God a name. But Hagar, this slave woman—raped, mistreated, unseen—has a face-to-face encounter with God, and she becomes the first person in the Bible to give God a name. What is the name she gives Him? El Roi—"the God who sees."

I don't dare to compare myself to Hagar—owned, raped, mistreated, unprotected—but I do want to share what my "unseen in the desert" moments can look like. It happens sometimes in the middle of the night. When it's 2:00 a.m. and I wake to my child, who faced some trigger that flipped their brain into a state of such fear that they lash out in every kind of violence toward themselves and toward me. My child is inches from my face: "I'm going to punch you right in the face. I hate you." They desperately bang on the second-story window, scream, "Neighbors! Call the police! Call the police so they take me away from this family!"

I sit in a dark room, back against the door, and tears stream down my face. And I think, *I'm all alone. How is this my life? They will never change; this will never change. I can't keep doing this.* I am no Hagar. But I am a mother with overwhelming feelings of fear and sadness, feeling unseen.

But it's in these times that I can experience the intimacy, the closeness, the all-seeing nature of El Roi. And as I remember that I am seen, my eyes are turned away from my circumstances, away from myself, and toward Him.

"I have now seen the One who sees me," said Hagar. God sees me. *God sees me.* And when I become aware that He sees me, it draws me into awe and worship that He would condescend to see me (because "what is man that you are mindful of him, and the son of man that you care for him?" [Ps. 8:4 ESV]), and it pulls my eyes back to seeing Him.

God sees me. And now I look back to Him, and I'm able to say, "I have now seen the One who sees me."

FURTHER READING

Genesis 16; 21:8–20

46

> Have I not commanded you? Be strong and
> courageous. Do not be frightened, and do
> not be dismayed, for the LORD your God is
> with you wherever you go.
>
> Joshua 1:9 ESV

I pulled up to the prison and double-checked the list given to me by the worker. No red (Bloods). No blue (Crips). No khaki (so as not to, you know, be confused with the prisoners). Borrowed bra (no underwire allowed). Single van key, no remote. License, no wallet. Absolutely nothing—not even a diaper—for the toddler in my arms. Fear in my heart.

This was all a bit scary, but it wasn't (just) the prison and its rules in and of themselves that scared me. It was the importance of this visit. I was meeting Dad for the first time. I had been parenting his child for years now, but she had seen him very few times, and I had never come face-to-face with him. My task—given to me by the worker and lawyer—was to plead with Dad to sign his parental rights away so that they wouldn't have to *take* his parental rights away. There was simply no chance of him legally being allowed to parent her, and a certain and heartbreaking hearing approached if he didn't choose to sign.

I was patted down, locked in, and led to a waiting room with a guard outside it. I sat in silence with my foster daughter—unusual compared to our typical chattiness—and I began to pray. As I spoke to God through my fear, He spoke back to me through His Word, hidden in my heart: "Be strong and courageous. Do not be frightened, and do not be dismayed, for the

Lord your God is with you wherever you go" (v. 9 ESV). I said a quiet prayer of thanks for my mom, who'd tucked Bible stories and verses like this into my heart in childhood.

In the book of Joshua, Moses has recently died, and God's people are not yet settled in His promised land. The people are hard to lead, and the enemies with their ensuing battles are countless. A new leader needs to be installed, and God calls Joshua. The "coronation" is unmemorable compared to the command that follows: Be strong. Have courage. Don't be afraid.

But God, in His mercy, doesn't come with just a command. He comes with an encouragement, a hope-filled, faith-inducing promise: "I will be with you. I will not leave you or forsake you" (v. 5 ESV). God doesn't just tell Joshua what *he* should do; He emboldens Joshua with what *He—God*—will do.

Being alone can be scary, and the presence of another brings comfort in frightening situations. But God's presence isn't like another human's presence, driving away the scary sounds and shadows of nighttime with their nearness. His presence is about more than proximity; it's about power.

Why could Joshua be strong and courageous? Because the Lord, *who was with him*, would empower him to lead His people, miraculously hand him victory in battle, make him "prosperous and successful" (v. 8), and give him every place where he set his foot (v. 3). Why could I be strong and courageous? Because the Lord, *who was with me*, would comfort me while I sat in a prison visit room and give me the words to speak to my daughter's father. And beyond that day and its frightening chore, He would continue to be with me, redeeming and restoring my daughter's story and bringing about His loving, wise, and already ordained, good plan.

As I sat and waited, I began reciting my faith-filled mantra: *Be strong. Be courageous. The Lord is with you. And in His presence is power.*

FURTHER READING

Isaiah 41

47

May God himself, the God of peace, sanctify you through and through. May your whole spirit, soul and body be kept blameless at the coming of our Lord Jesus Christ.

1 Thessalonians 5:23

had already learned my lesson. After entering foster care with the sole intention of protecting kids, I had gained a heart for their parents also. I started off believing that adoption was the very best outcome of any foster placement and grew to understand that reunification—a family being restored—was an even better one. This led me to want to be a part of that, to do everything I could to support the family unit before and after reunification. My new definition of success: a parent and child reunified, and me standing alongside them before *and after*.

Someone once came up to me at an event for foster parents that I was speaking at and said, "You're that 'pro-bio-family' foster mom, aren't you? Yeah, I unfollowed you." Rude, but okay. I would wear that as a badge of honor. *Yeah, I'm that pro-bio-family foster mom*. I liked being known that way, even if it meant one less follower.

My kiddo was ready to head home. I had supported Mom and reunification throughout the placement—relationally, practically, and sacrificially—and I was ready to keep doing it afterward. I was going to be Mom's support network. We had a plan, and we made a schedule. And then the kiddo reunified and the contact dropped off. No more daily phone calls, no more "co-parenting" this child, no offers for visits or contact—all things I had offered throughout placement and had been offered in return.

But I am that pro-bio-family foster mom! My picture of foster care success is a happy mom and child and me—*me!*—standing alongside them before *and after*. This was not the achievement I'd planned it would be. This was a different plan from the one I had concocted. This wasn't a win.

Thank God that He, in His grace, doesn't leave us where we are. He convicts us, teaches us, grows us, transforms us. I thought that I had done all the changing that needed to be done. I used to make foster care about me getting a kid, and now I was making it about them getting their family. I learned my lesson, right? But my self-centered, self-exalting, self-interested—*self*—was still making it about me. Though I wouldn't have ever said it so explicitly, I wanted my plan to happen. I wanted the continued relationship I felt I had earned, I wanted to experience the joy of staying involved in serving them, and I wanted the recognition for doing so. I wanted people to see me as *that pro-bio-family foster mom*.

Sometimes God allows hard things—even ordains hard things—to sanctify us through and through. John Piper defines sanctification as "progressively becoming like Jesus."* It is the process through which we partner with the Holy Spirit to grow in holiness. And God is more committed to this process than we could ever be.

More than our passing comfort, God wants our "whole spirit, soul and body [to] be kept blameless" (v. 23). He loves us

---

*John Piper, "Sanctification: So Why the Long Word?," Desiring God, accessed July 31, 2023, https://www.desiringgod.org/articles/sanctification-so-why-the -long-word.

enough to be singularly committed to making us more like Him by any means necessary. Not because He is an exacting dictator but because He is a loving Father. Our holiness and happiness are intertwined because His best for us is always found in Him.

I thought I had "arrived" as a foster parent, but God had some sanctifying to do. He needed to increase, and I needed to decrease (John 3:30), and He was going to allow me to walk through something painful to bring about something good in me. Friend, we can trust Him to do that because "He who began a good work in [us] will bring it to completion" (Phil. 1:6 ESV).

FURTHER READING

John 17

48

Look, I am coming soon! My reward is with
me, and I will give to each person according to what they have done.

Revelation 22:12

Sometimes the Bible has a funny way of getting its point
across. See, for instance, the dozens of verses that talk
about how ridiculously short and passing our lives are.
"What is your life?" James 4:14 asks in a hilariously insulting
manner. "For you are a mist that appears for a little time and then
vanishes" (ESV). Other verses declare that "man is like a breath;
his days are like a passing shadow" (Ps. 144:4 ESV), and "all flesh
is like grass" (1 Pet. 1:24 ESV). David bemoans that his "days are
like an evening shadow" (Ps. 102:11 ESV) and his "lifetime is as
nothing before [God]" (Ps. 39:5 ESV).

These Scriptures use many different pictures to get one idea
across: Your life is quick and it is passing. Maybe this seems de-
pressing to you, but I find great comfort in this truth. Foster care
feels long and hard. You know, "the days are long, but the years
are short"? Yeah, well, foster care turns even that on its head.
The days are long *and* the years are long. The fact that "the world
is passing away along with its desires" (1 John 2:17 ESV) puts into
perspective the things we sacrifice as foster parents. And the
reality that the hard days of foster care, the ones that feel heavy
and like they go on forever, are actually "light and momentary"
(2 Cor. 4:17) gives context to the hard we're walking through.

Within the verses that celebrate the brevity of our lives,
we find a hidden invitation, a too-good-to-refuse investment

opportunity. When we recognize that we are (take your pick) breath, shadow, grass, or—my favorite—"nothing" (Ps. 39:5), we are freed *from* living like these short days are all there is and *to* living for heaven, which will go on and on forever.

"Look, I am coming soon!" exclaims Jesus, "My reward is with me, and I will give to each person according to what they have done" (Rev. 22:12). What have you done, for kids, families, your community, as a foster parent? How have you sacrificed your own joy, your own time, your own family for the good of a stranger? Well, "God is not unjust; he will not forget your work and the love you have shown him as you have helped his people and continue to help them" (Heb. 6:10). God calls Himself a rewarder (11:6), and He entices us with promises of thrilling, eternal rewards. Inheritance, crown, glory, commendation, reward, harvest, treasure, prize, and repayment are just a few of the things He says we can look forward to.* Friend, read those words again! God wants you to be motivated by the eternal gifts that He promises to give you for the work He's called you to do!

Living out our days in sacrificial love for Jesus and people is, simply put, an investment opportunity, an invitation to trade in what is passing away for what will last forever. "He is no fool who gives what he cannot keep to gain what he cannot lose," said Jim Elliot (before he quite literally gave everything to bring the hope of Jesus to those without access to the gospel).** When we are aware that these days of ours are short and passing away anyway, we can have vision for the great exchange of living them for eternity. There is a glorious trade in that we are

---

*inheritance (Col. 3:23–24), crown (James 1:12), glory (2 Cor. 4:17), commendation (Matt. 25:23), reward (1 Cor. 3:8), harvest (Gal. 6:9), treasure (Matt. 6:20), prize (1 Cor. 9:24), repayment (Rev. 22:12)

**Quoted in Elisabeth Elliot, *Through Gates of Splendor* (Carol Stream, IL: Tyndale House, 1986), 172.

offered by God to take something that won't last, something we're going to lose anyway, and spend it up for what will last forever.

He will "give to each person according to what they've done." I want to live for *that* day.

FURTHER READING

Revelation 22; *In Light of Eternity* by Randy Alcorn

49

For who sees anything different in you?
What do you have that you did not receive? If then you received it, why do you
boast as if you did not receive it?

1 Corinthians 4:7 ESV

Her face was hard and unfriendly peeking through her hijab. With her hair and body completely covered by her traditional Muslim garb, there was nothing else to evaluate her by than her face. And it was hard. And unfriendly. *Well, hello to you too.*

She watched me walk into the doctor's office with the baby—her baby—in my arms and didn't make a move. No effort to say hello, no attempt to connect with her baby. *What kind of mom doesn't even want to see her kid?* They brought us back immediately, before I could sit or say hi, so our first meeting was alone in the small, silent exam room.

"Hi." I smiled. "I know this is super awkward! But I'm happy we get to meet because your daughter is just so special. Here! Do you want to hold her?"

"Thank you," she said as her "hard" and "unfriendly" face broke into a big smile. Her voice was so sweet and soft, she sounded like a child—because she was a child. She cuddled and kissed her daughter as I asked her a few basic questions. Without breaking eye contact with her baby for a moment, she used my searching as an opportunity to open up about her life. It was broken and heartbreaking. Dad left her for another woman right before the baby came along, leaving her homeless. Grandma passed, Grandpa serving for drug charges, no one in the world to step in.

The picture I'd created of a hard, unfriendly woman who didn't care about her baby dissolved into the actual sweet, scared, doting mama before my eyes. As I compared her life and family and experiences to my own, I was pierced with the conviction, *How are you any better than anyone else? What do you have that wasn't given to you anyway? And if it was only a gift, why are you arrogant as though you deserve it?* (my paraphrase of 1 Cor. 4:7).

As Christians, we should be the very humblest of people.

We know who we are: sinners (Rom. 3:23).

We know what we deserve: death (Rom. 6:23).

We know what we've been given: life and salvation (Eph. 2:8; 1 John 5:11).

And still we—myself at the front of the pack—see others through a lens of self-righteousness and arrogance. *Why don't you . . . ? How could you . . . ? Why can't you . . . ?*

I challenge you, as I do myself: "Do not think of yourself more highly than you ought, but rather think of yourself with sober judgment" (Rom. 12:3).

Do not forget the list of blessings and privileges that have made up your life. Do not forget the second chances you've received, the people who've carried you and cared for you, the gifts given you from others and from the hand of God. Do not forget, your very life and breath themselves are a moment-by-moment gift of God. And do not forget, most of all, the greatest, most undeserved gift you've received: the Savior Himself. "For it is by grace you have been saved, through faith—and this is not from yourselves, it is the gift of God—not by works, so that no one can boast" (Eph. 2:8–9).

Your forgiveness and salvation, your life and breath, your home and family and mental health and support system and every ounce of every single thing is all a gift from God. May you live and love, always, as if you are someone who's received much and love with the humility that brings.

FURTHER READING

1 Peter 5

50

And we know that in all things God works for
the good of those who love him, who have
been called according to his purpose. . . .

If God is for us, who can be against us? He
who did not spare his own Son, but gave him up
for us all—how will he not also, along with him,
graciously give us all things?

Romans 8:28, 31–32

"All the things." It's become a phrase that encapsulates everything without having to define it all. I could tell you all that makes up my mental worry list: *Is three months of being clean really long enough to know if she can stay clean? What if he doesn't outgrow smearing poop and is still doing it as an adult? The principal probably thinks she learned that terrible word she wrote on the bathroom wall at home. What if the therapist doesn't write the note she promised she'd write? Did that aunt's boyfriend actually move out, or is he still in the house with the baby?* Or I could just wrap it all up in one carefree, catchall phrase: "I'm just feeling the weight of *all the things*."

There are so many burdens and worries and fears and hopes that a foster mom carries on her heart and mind—*all the things*. Romans 8:28 offers hope to this burdened heart.

Paul assures us with the nearly unbelievable promise that for God's children who love Him and have been called, He works *all things* for good. *All things* means *all the things*. All the things that we carry and worry over and try to control. All the things that we're sure there can be no possible good in, that we're certain no good could possibly come from.

Paul knows how too good to be true this promise appears, so he backs it with the reminder of something even more unbelievable: the incredible—*and already fulfilled*—promise of the very Son of God Himself for our salvation! "He who did not spare his own Son, but gave him up for us all—how will he not also, along with him, graciously give us all things?" he asks (v. 32), leading us to the only logical conclusion: Of course He will give us all things! We have many needs, and we feel the weight of them all, but these weighty earthly needs *pale* in comparison to our most pressing need—for rescue, forgiveness, salvation. Your greatest need, my greatest need—most desperate, most impossible, and *already taken care of*—was met when Jesus died for us.

We come to our Father with all the things and wonder if He can handle them. Our hearts question—whether we let it slip through our lips or not—if He is strong enough, present enough, good enough to do *even this*. And in doing so, we forget the evidence of His strength and presence and goodness in what He's already done.

Our God is a God so great and so good that He didn't even spare His own Son for us. Will He not also—along with His very Son—graciously give us all things? He gave us Jesus. We can trust Him for everything else.

FURTHER READING

Romans 8

51

For the LORD is our judge; the LORD is our
   lawgiver;
the LORD is our king.

Isaiah 33:22 ESV

was called to the stand. I want to say I put my hand on a
Bible and did the whole "tell the truth, the whole truth, and
nothing but the truth" thing, but I can't promise that this
would be a true memory and not a movie-induced invention.
But I definitely sat on the stand, I definitely did some kind of
swearing, and I was definitely examined and cross-examined. It's
the cross-examination that's frightening. The first lawyer—the
one I knew, the one who prepared me—that one was cake, but
the second? Their job was to trip me up, to confuse me, to win.
I (proverbially and quite literally) sweated the whole thing, but
came out pretty much unscathed. All I had to do was answer
their questions honestly. I knew what I knew about this child,
about what had happened, and I would testify to it. This trial
was about piecing it all together in pursuit of truth, in pursuit of
justice.

God cares deeply about justice. "The LORD is our judge"
(33:22) and "all his ways are justice" (Deut. 32:4 ESV). His
righteousness—His inherent *rightness*—and His justice are central to His character. He "loves the just" (Ps. 37:28), and He calls
his people to love and pursue justice. He tells us to "hold fast to
love and justice" (Hos. 12:6 ESV), to "act justly" (Mic. 6:8), and
to "learn to do right [and] seek justice" (Isa. 1:17).

But as foster parents, we see firsthand how foster care swells with injustice—toward the children, toward biological families, toward us. We stand in the middle of this system appointed to uphold justice and see it swelling with unfairness and corruption and lack.

This is why my hope is not in the honorable Judge So-and-So. It is in the fulfillment of honor, righteousness, and justice Himself. I don't trust the system, but I trust the One above the system. "I know that [He] can do all things" and that "no purpose of [His] can be thwarted" (Job 42:2), and I trust His good plan, even when it seems like those making the plans are not good. The Sovereign Judge assigns authority to the "governing authorities"—namely, the judges and players in the system—to accomplish His will. So I "submit" to the earthly judge out of "reverent fear of God" (1 Pet. 2:18), knowing that I'm actually submitting to Him, the heavenly Judge. I remember that "the king's heart is a stream of water in the hand of the Lord; he turns it wherever he will" (Prov. 21:1 ESV), and He uses even broken leaders and systems to bring about His plan.

Jesus spoke to the man who was handing Him over to be killed: "You would have no authority over me at all unless it had been given you from above" (John 19:11 ESV). And when He could have called on His Father to "put at [His] disposal more than twelve legions of angels" (Matt. 26:53) to rescue Him, He submitted to His own crucifixion. This cosmic injustice was the will of the Father (Mark 14:36), and through Jesus's death, justice was fulfilled (Rom. 3:23–26) and our redemption was won. *This* is why I trust and believe and know that the Just Judge wins. As I sit in the in-between, watching a system that hurts kids and families and watching injustice "win," I cry out, "How long will the wicked triumph?" (Ps. 94:3 NKJV). But I know and cling to the answer: "God will bring into judgment both the righteous and the wicked, for there will be a time for every activity, a time to judge every deed" (Eccles. 3:17).

"For we know him who said, 'Vengeance is mine; I will repay'" (Heb. 10:30 ESV), and our hope is in His perfect justice.

FURTHER READING

Romans 3:23–26; Psalm 37

52

I can do all things through him who strengthens me. . . .

And my God will supply every need of yours according to his riches in glory in Christ Jesus. To our God and Father be glory forever and ever. Amen.

Philippians 4:13, 19–20 ESV

I said yes to a placement call yesterday. I've said yes quite a few times over the past couple of weeks, but each time we ended up not being needed. We'd get the initial call, but then a family member would be found or another situation worked out. I've come to learn that this is how most of our yeses play out, so they feel less weighty in the moment. This time, we got the follow-up call—the "he's really coming" call.

So last night I did what any veteran foster parent and mission-focused disciple of Jesus would do. I lay in bed and tried to concoct a story that would get me out of having to actually accept the placement without looking bad to the worker. You want the authentic confessions of a foster parent? There it is.

Anxiety had taken over my heart. I've done this many times before, and I know what it will entail. We will be uprooting our rhythms, changing our routines, threatening the delicate balance that is our family system. This being our thirtieth placement, I know exactly what's at stake, and when I consider it all, the most prevailing feeling is the need to escape.

It begs the question: Is the feat in front of me greater than the God who called me to it? Or do I really believe that my God will supply all my needs? Do I believe that I can truly do all things through Him who gives me strength? "His divine power has given us everything we need for a godly life through our knowledge of him who called us" (2 Pet. 1:3).

My natural needs are lofty and large until they are shrunk down to their rightful, doable size by the supernatural power of God—the Need Supplier and Strength Giver Himself. My fears aren't going to be assuaged by my genius ten-step plan or a new and improved schedule. They are going to be answered by looking away from myself, my abilities, and my needs and looking to my God.

And where does my confidence for this land? In the "riches of his glory in Christ Jesus" (Phil. 4:19) from which my needs are met. Paul points to the cross of Christ—the place where Jesus defeated sin and death—as the confidence builder for our assurance that He will meet our needs and give us the ability to do all things. "The immeasurable greatness of his power toward us who believe, according to the working of his great might that he worked in Christ when he raised him from the dead" (Eph. 1:19–20 ESV). This power that raised Christ from the dead is the same power directed toward us. It is an impossible, life-from-death kind of power, and it is at work in our lives.

To the glory of our God and Father—which all of this is about anyway—forever and ever. Amen.

Note: To be clear, sometimes the answer shouldn't be yes; sometimes it should be a resounding no. Reread the Day 20 devotion for more on that.

FURTHER READING

2 Corinthians 13

53

God is our refuge and strength,
an ever-present help in trouble.

Psalm 46:1

_____

She has parental visits four times a week. She doesn't like going on visits. They're held in a 10' × 10' windowless room with dirty linoleum floors and a couple of old toys and books. Dad slides his chair into the doorway, pulls out his phone, and strikes up a conversation with the woman doing the same, the next room over.

She has a new worker supervising her visits. This new worker is a man. She is terrified of men. When my brother, with his booming voice, enters our home, she hides in the felt safety of the empty kitchen cabinet and pulls the door closed. When we sit at a restaurant and the male server approaches, her body shakes in terror and she looks down so deeply that her nose nearly touches the table. The prospect of a man coming to our home, taking her from my arms, buckling her in his car while she screams, and driving away is heartbreaking. Knowing there won't be anyone comforting and nurturing her once she arrives is even worse.

I believe in visits. I believe they are an important point of connection for a child and parent. I believe they can allow a mom or dad to receive the parenting coaching they need. I believe they're important for a child's sense of identity and belonging. I believe they are an opportunity to remind a parent, _This is who you're fighting for!_

I believe in visits. And sometimes, I hate them. I hate the continued trauma—trauma on trauma. This broken system, serving broken families, made up of broken people, has brokenness present in every nook of it. And while I don't lie down in defeat, I surrender to the place I'm slotted to hold in this arrangement. I get her ready and pack her bag and send her off screaming with a strange man to visit with a just-a-little-bit-less-strange man, her father.

When my kiddo is sad and scared and struggling, there's nothing more I want than to be there and make it better for them. *They need me*, I conclude. *I am the one who can make this okay. I am the only one.*

But when I speak this—or simply claim it in my heart—I am forgetting another One altogether. Because while I believe my presence would comfort and help, my presence is nothing compared to His. "The LORD your God is with you wherever you go," says Joshua 1:9 (ESV), and with Him there, who needs me?

While I struggle to remain present even in the space I hold, He is an "ever-present help" (Ps. 46:1). While I grapple with knowing what they need, He is able to give everything in His perfect wisdom (Rom. 11:33). While my love is imperfect, His love is flawless (1 John 4:18) and never-ending (Jer. 31:3). While I am weak and limited, He is a refuge and strength (Ps. 46:1).

Don't get me wrong, I advocate for visits to be different, for her to be better supported and nurtured. But when my advocating falls on the deaf ears of workers, I know my prayers are heard and answered by my God. I know that He is supernaturally and automatically able to bring comfort to my kids that my own limited proximity and language could never provide. I know that when I cannot be there, He is, and His presence is effectual to bring them all that they need. I know that He can divinely provide peace to their bodies, comfort to their hearts, and quiet to their minds in a way that circumvents every one of my human limitations completely.

My paltry parenting abilities pale before the heavenly Father's perfect Fatherhood. My kids are far better off in His hands than they could ever be in mine, so why would I try to wrestle them from His more capable arms?

As I place her in the arms of the worker, I am actually entrusting her into the arms of the Father. And what I believe *for* her, what I believe *about* Him, is that He is her refuge, her strength, and her ever-present help in trouble.

FURTHER READING

Psalm 46

54

I have told you these things, so that in me you may have peace. In this world you will have trouble. But take heart! I have overcome the world.

John 16:33

We love to claim the promises of God. Scripture is full of words from and about God that bolster our hearts with hope and joy. "I will never leave you nor forsake you" (Heb. 13:5 ESV). "For those who love God all things work together for good" (Rom. 8:28 ESV). These Scriptures are bold and beautiful truths that we should build our hearts upon, but I've got another, very different kind of promise for you. Ready? "You will have trouble" (John 16:33).

Jesus is about to be arrested. He knows His hour is coming, so He gathers His friends and prays for them and speaks His final words to them. He promises the Holy Spirit, reminds them of "the Way," and speaks of His love. But it's not a happy-go-lucky pep talk. He tells them that they will be hated (15:18–19), they will be persecuted (v. 20), they will be thrown out of the gathering of God's people, their very lives will be threatened (16:2), and they will grieve (v. 20). His very final words to His disciples, whom He loves, are words of warning. "I have said all these things to you to keep you from falling away," He tells them (v. 1 ESV). He doesn't want their hearts to be troubled when they face the trouble that is sure to come (14:1).

I'm rather certain "You will have trouble" has occupied far fewer embroidery rings than its more hopeful counterparts, and you're probably not tattooing it on your ankle. But I find it encouraging. Because let me tell you, if it weren't for these trouble-promising words, I would be certain that I was doing something wrong. *I followed you into this mission of loving and serving the orphaned and vulnerable, God. Shouldn't this be easier? Aren't there supposed to be blessings and favor? Isn't this supposed to be going a little bit better?*

My home is full of a lot of joy and love—it is. But this promise of trouble, well, it resonates. I've given you my list so many times in the pages of this book. I'd encourage you to stop for a moment and think of your own. Catalog for a moment the kids and parents and workers, the goodbyes and court days and behaviors. Remember the weaknesses, insults, hardships, persecutions, and difficulties (2 Cor. 12:10). Think about it, and then remember: He has overcome it all.

Overcome means to "defeat" or "overwhelm."* For the spaces of this foster care journey that need to be defeated—the darkness, the trauma, the abuse, the injustice—"thanks be to God, who gives us the victory through our Lord Jesus Christ" (1 Cor. 15:57 ESV). And for the spaces that need to be overwhelmed—the hopelessness, the hardship, the fear, the heartache—He offers a peace that "surpasses all understanding" (Phil. 4:7 ESV) and "unfailing love" (Ps. 86:15 NLT) that engulfs our hearts.

As it is now, trouble doesn't *look* overcome. But this claim of overcoming isn't an eventual, one-day kind of promise ("I *will* overcome the world"); it's an all-done, already-won kind of promise ("I *have* overcome the world"). Theologians call this the "already but not yet" of waiting and watching what God already did to be fully, completely revealed. Our troubles, though

---

*Oxford Language Dictionary, s.v. "overcome (v.)," accessed January 1, 2024, https://www.oed.com/search/dictionary/?scope=Entries&q=overcome.

they remain, have already been overcome. They will not have the final word, they will not defeat, they will not win. So, in the midst of walking through them, we find the peace of "taking heart" and knowing that we are waiting to watch how He has already overcome.

FURTHER READING

John 15–16

55

Then came one of the rulers of the synagogue, Jairus by name, and seeing [Jesus], he fell at his feet and implored him earnestly, saying, "My little daughter is at the point of death. Come and lay your hands on her, so that she may be made well and live." And he went with him. . . .

There came from the ruler's house some who said, "Your daughter is dead. Why trouble the Teacher any further?" But overhearing what they said, Jesus said to the ruler of the synagogue, "Do not fear, only believe." . . . Taking her by the hand he said to her, "Talitha cumi," which means, "Little girl, I say to you, arise." And immediately the girl got up and began walking (for she was twelve years of age), and they were immediately overcome with amazement.

Mark 5:22–24, 35–36, 41–42 ESV

I was reading a book by Dr. Bruce Perry and Oprah Winfrey called *What Happened to You?* when I came across truly shocking research. "If, in the first two months of life, a child experienced high adversity with minimal relational buffering but then was put into a healthier environment for the next twelve years, their outcomes were worse than the outcomes of children who had low adversity and healthy relational connection in the first two months but then spent the next twelve years with high adversity."* Or, in other words, the first sixty days of a child's life are more crucial to development than *any other time*. If a baby experiences trauma within the first two months of their life, the effects are even more pervasive and devastating than if they experienced over a decade of abuse as an older child.

This research is heart-wrenching to any mother who missed the first days, weeks, or months with her child, especially if she knows that child experienced adversity—neglect, chaos, medical trauma, abuse. Reading something like this can feel like a life sentence. *This child's "outcomes" were predetermined before I even met them. I'm too late. There's no hope.*

Jairus's daughter was facing a death sentence. Faced with a hopeless situation, he ran to the Savior in hope. He fell at Jesus's feet and called out in faith, "Come and lay your hands on her, so that she may be made well and live" (v. 23).

So, Jesus goes with him to her, but on the road to Jairus's home, they are met with a final message: He is too late. Jesus calls Jairus to hold fast to the faith that drove him to Jesus's feet. "Do not fear, only believe" (v. 36). And then Jesus enters the room of the dead child, takes her by the hand, and brings her back to life.

There are two things that I believe simultaneously and completely. First, the effects of trauma on the brains, bodies, biology, beliefs, and behaviors of the children in our care are pervasive and devastating. Second, God can and does heal.

I believe it's important to hold these beliefs simultaneously in order to be both faith*ful* and faith-*filled* parents. There are many books on trauma-informed parenting. I've read many of them,

---

*Erin P. Hambrick, Thomas W. Brawner, Bruce D. Perry, "Timing of Early-Life Stress and the Development of Brain-Related Capacities," *Frontiers in Behavioral Neuroscience* 13 (August 6, 2019): 183, https://doi.org/10.3389/fnbeh.2019.00183.

and I hope you do. But may we never be so consumed with helping our children find healing that we forget to fall at the feet of the Great Healer.

Do you believe that Jesus made the blind see, the deaf hear, the lame walk, and *took the hands of dead little girls and brought them back to life*? Do you believe that He is the same yesterday, today, and forever? Do you believe that this Savior can heal your child?

Maybe for some, healing will be miraculous and instantaneous, like a little girl raised back to life. I think for most, healing will be long fought for, slowly won, and incomplete while on this earth. But for all, may we hear the Savior's words, "Do not fear, only believe," and may we hold tight to them. May we run to Jesus and plead for our children's healing; may we throw off fear and cling to belief in Him, the Great Healer.

FURTHER READING

John 9

56

And he who was seated on the throne
said, "Behold, I am making all things new."
Also he said, "Write this down, for these
words are trustworthy and true."

Revelation 21:5 ESV

We had said goodbye to our foster daughter after two
and a half years of her being in our home. To say that
I was heartbroken would be an understatement. But
I was also rejoicing that she was with her mom. But I was also
heartbroken. *And* I was rejoicing . . . well, you get it.

Coming into worship on a Sunday morning often leaves
me particularly emotionally vulnerable. The music, while loud,
quiets the noise of the usual voices and tasks and—as music
was created by the Creator to do—pulls viscerally on my frag-
ile emotions. I'm not content to sing words to Him that I don't
mean, so singing becomes a battle within my heart to lay claim
to the lyrics I'm declaring. I'm praising and wrestling and fighting
and rejoicing. Worship is a time when I'm laid bare before my
Father—mind, body, and spirit.

> All glory be to Christ our King,
> All glory be to Christ.
> His rule and reign we'll ever sing,
> All glory be to Christ.

The drums build and echo the pounding of my heart as we
crescendo into the final verse—the verse about heaven.

When on the day, the great I Am,
the faithful and the true,
The Lamb who was for sinners slain,
*is making all things new.**

I broke. Tears streamed down my face, my chest heaved and my shoulders shook. I didn't cry. I wept. My thoughts and prayers had been back and forth between grieving our good-bye and cheering her reunification, reeling from our loss and rejoicing in their gain, mourning what our family once was and celebrating what their family had become. It was always them on one side, us on the other. One emotion or the opposite. But someone was always "losing."

These words and the music paired with them pulled my heart into seeing what I had actually, truly, deep down been craving: for all things to be made new.

I didn't want her to be with me and not her mom. I didn't want her to be with her mom and not me. She was experiencing the grief, the loss, the brokenness of it all, no matter who she was with. What I wanted was a world without grief, without loss, without brokenness.

The heartbreak I was walking through in this life gave me a craving for the next life. "He has put eternity into man's heart" (Eccles. 3:11 ESV), and I was feeling the tug of eternity. I was feeling the pull toward things being made right and whole, things re-becoming new. A time when "the old order of things has passed away" and there is finally "no more death or mourning or crying or pain." I was craving the day when "He will wipe every tear from [our] eyes" (Rev. 21:4) and everything sad will come untrue.

---

*"All Glory Be to Christ," words by Dustin Kensrue, performed by Kings Kaleidoscope on *Joy Has Dawned*, Mars Hill Music, 2012. Used by permission.

No matter what you're walking through as a foster parent, simply put, it was not supposed to be this way. Children hurt, families torn apart, the devastating effects of sin—this is the "old" of the brokenness of this world. But there is a God, seated on the throne, King of heaven and of earth, and He declares, "Forget the former things; do not dwell on the past. See, I am doing a new thing!" (Isa. 43:18–19).

FURTHER READING

Revelation 21

57

You intended to harm me, but God intended it for good to accomplish what is now being done, the saving of many lives.

Genesis 50:20

I will do my best to summarize Genesis 37–50, the story of Joseph, in under ten sentences. Basically, Dad chooses Joseph as the very favorite of all his sons. This, combined with the fact that Joseph has prophetic dreams of his brothers worshiping him *and* the poor sense to share these dreams with his brothers, makes them all (kind of understandably) hate him. They talk about killing him but decide to instead throw him in a pit, sell him into slavery in Egypt, and provide Dad with a blood-soaked technicolor dream coat as proof of his farce of a death. In Egypt, Joseph is falsely accused of rape and unjustly imprisoned. There he interprets a few dreams for a few formerly important people but is left forgotten and languishing in prison for years. That is, until the day he's brought up to interpret the pharaoh's dreams. The dreams are not good news (skinny cows and withering corn stalks are, apparently, omens of famine and death), but because Joseph deciphers the secret message and comes up with a plan, Pharaoh makes him his right-hand man. When the whole skinny-cow, withering-corn thing comes true and the world actually begins starving, Dad sends his brood of sons to Egypt to buy food, where (*gasp!*) they come face-to-face with their once-hated little brother turned Egyptian ruler. And now we're up to speed. (Eight sentences, thank you very much.)

We talk about "broken families" in the context of foster care. Well, Joseph knows all about broken families. Joseph's story includes a murder plot, parental loss, slavery, and false accusations. He suffers through betrayal and loneliness and waiting and sorrow.

When Joseph is finally face-to-face with his murderous brothers again, he has not only the access but also the authority to exact his revenge. But when it comes down to it, his response is not what you expect. After many years of suffering, Joseph looks at his brothers, who were responsible for all of his pain, and says, "You may have had an evil plan, but God had a good plan—for me and all the lives I would save, including yours—all along" (Gen. 50:20, my paraphrase).

Did Joseph respond this way because, in the end, he was rich and powerful and on top? Maybe. Was it because he was a super-forgiving guy who didn't hold grudges? Possibly. But his response is clear that, above all, Joseph held a deep trust in the sovereignty of God over all things, even the evil actions and intentions of others. He knew that even his brothers' plans to hurt him were ultimately God's plans to help him and to help others through him.

How can we be "okay" with parents and players in the system who have brought harm to our children? How can we have peace when considering what our kids have experienced (or not experienced and should have)? We remember that *nothing* is outside the control of our God.

Our God is sovereign. He "works all things according to the counsel of his will" (Eph. 1:11 ESV) and "no purpose of [His] can be thwarted" (Job 42:2). But He isn't just sovereign; "He is good [and] his steadfast love endures forever" (Ps. 118:1 ESV). He is the "only wise God" (Rom. 16:27), whose "ways [are] higher than your ways and [His] thoughts than your thoughts"

(Isa. 55:9). His sovereignty and power ensure that He is in control and can do *any*thing, and His wisdom and love ensure that He is good and will do the *right* thing.

In foster care, we will be exposed to the brokenness of family and the evil intentions and actions of others, but we are under the caring control of a wise and loving God. He is always willing and working to accomplish His good plan, so we can trust Him. "The purpose of the LORD . . . will stand" (Prov. 19:21 ESV).

FURTHER READING

Romans 9:6–29; 11:33–36

58

God is not man, that he should lie,
   or a son of man, that he should change his
      mind.
Has he said, and will he not do it?
   Or has he spoken, and will he not fulfill it?

Numbers 23:19 ESV

There is a shared language among foster parents. It goes something like this:

"He was supposed to be a 'weekend respite,' but that was nine months ago."

"She told me that she would put the referral in, but I'll believe it when I see it."

"Mom said she's really going to leave him this time, but she's said that five times before."

"The judge said if they didn't have the paperwork next time, he would hold them in contempt, but he always threatens to hold them accountable and never does."

Behind each of these statements—and the hundreds of others I've said and heard just like them—is one foundational understanding: People say things that don't end up being true. Maybe they're lying, maybe they're powerless to deliver as promised, maybe they change their minds. But they don't do it, they don't fulfill it, and it leaves us mistrustful of the system and disbelieving of the people.

But we can't put God in this promise-breaking majority. "For all the promises of God find their Yes in him" (2 Cor. 1:20 ESV), and "He who promised is faithful" (Heb. 10:23). God is the perfect Promise Maker and Keeper, and we can place our full trust in every word He's spoken to us.

What promise do you need to believe as if it is really, fully true?

Maybe it's for your child:

- "The LORD your God is with you wherever you go" (Josh. 1:9 ESV).
- "The LORD is good to all, and His tender mercies are over all His works" (Ps. 145:9 NKJV).

Maybe it's for their family:

- "He tends his flock like a shepherd: He gathers the lambs in his arms and carries them close to his heart; he gently leads those that have young" (Isa. 40:11).
- "Jesus looked at them and said, 'With man this is impossible, but with God all things are possible'" (Matt. 19:26).

Maybe it's for yourself:

- "I am your God; I will strengthen you, I will help you, I will uphold you with my righteous right hand" (Isa. 41:10 ESV).
- "I will give you rest. . . . You will find rest for your souls" (Matt. 11:28–29).

You can believe Him. You can hold Him to His word. You can stake your joy and peace and life itself on His claims. His promises are not like the "promises" of the lawyer, the case-worker, the parent—broken and unfulfilled. "Has he said, and will he not do it?" (Num. 23:19 ESV). Friend, believe me. Believe Him. He most certainly will.

FURTHER READING

Hebrews 6

59

I will say of the LORD, "He is my refuge and my
fortress,
my God, in whom I trust." . . .
He will cover you with his feathers,
and under his wings you will find refuge;
his faithfulness will be your shield and
rampart. . . .
For he will command his angels concerning you
to guard you in all your ways;
they will lift you up in their hands.

Psalm 91:2, 4, 11–12

My biological daughter was born by C-section. This was not the plan. The plan was a water birth at a birth center, after which my newborn baby, still tethered by the umbilical cord, would be placed on my chest, where she would crawl to my breast and effortlessly latch on and begin nursing. (I know it sounds fake, but this is an actual thing. You can Google it.)

Alas, I didn't get my water birth. I got an OR, a recovery room, bright-white lights, and bustling bodies. They brought my daughter up to my face for a quick look before whisking her away. "Go with her!" I commanded my husband.

"She's fine; they're taking good care of her," he responded.

"Go. With. Her," I demanded even more forcefully. It took me about four minutes of motherhood to be pushed to my mama-bear stage.

Sure, these were fully trained and well-vetted medical professionals, but I was not just going to trust my daughter—my child—with a stranger. I was a mother now, and my job was to *ensure* my child was okay. If this were a TV show, right about now would be when the record would scratch, symbolizing a dramatic and unexpected turn of events. Because this first moment of motherhood would be the first of many—and I mean *very many*—times that I haven't been able to keep my children under my watchful eye, my protective care, my *control*.

I've placed kids into the arms of workers, therapists, doctors, and nurses. I've had their clinging arms pulled from my neck as they've been handed over to strung-out mothers, shackled fathers, unwilling grandmothers and grandfathers, and unknown aunts and uncles. I've buckled them into cars that drove them away, forever, to people and places that were anything but what I would have chosen for them. I've learned—unwillingly, painfully, contrary to choice—what it means to surrender.

Being a foster parent has taught me how to love deeply and hold loosely, how to relinquish control, how to trust God. I've had to make the decision—once and for all and then again each day—to entrust my children to God. I've had to learn to take my heart to task, to "say of the Lord, 'He is my refuge and my fortress, my God, in whom I trust'" (v. 2).

When I cannot keep them under my watchful eye, I know that "The Lord will watch over [their] coming and going both now and forevermore" (121:8). When I cannot keep them in my protective care, I know that "He will command his angels concerning [them] to guard [them]" (91:11). When I am not in control, I know that "As [He has] planned, so shall it be, and as [He has] purposed, so shall it stand" (Isa. 14:24 ESV).

The mama-bear instinct is given by God and not easily overcome. Everything in me believes that my kids are better off with me than they would be anywhere else, so it takes the practice of reminding myself, saying of the Lord great and glorious truths about His protection, His control, His goodness. I remind myself of just Who it is I am entrusting my children to, and I find surrender in keeping them in His perfect care.

FURTHER READING

Psalm 18

60

As Jesus and his disciples were on their way, he came to a village where a woman named Martha opened her home to him. She had a sister called Mary, who sat at the Lord's feet listening to what he said. But Martha was distracted by all the preparations that had to be made. She came to him and asked, "Lord, don't you care that my sister has left me to do the work by myself? Tell her to help me!"

"Martha, Martha," the Lord answered, "you are worried and upset about many things, but few things are needed—or indeed only one. Mary has chosen what is better, and it will not be taken away from her."

Luke 10:38–42

Hospitality is a consistent ethic throughout the New Testament. "Do not neglect to show hospitality to strangers" (Heb. 13:2 ESV); "Show hospitality to one another" (1 Pet. 4:9 ESV); "Contribute to the needs of the saints and seek to show hospitality" (Rom. 12:13 ESV), Scripture exhorts. God doesn't want just our hearts and lives; He wants our homes.

Foster care is the pinnacle of hospitality. Opening the doors of your home and the bonds of your family to invite another person in—not only to reside with you but to become one of you—is the culmination of gospel hospitality. And inviting people into your home takes time and effort and energy. It takes feeding and clothing, communicating, and connecting. It takes "preparations," so to speak.

I can relate to Martha. I like to be a follower of Jesus who *does*. I like the busyness, the task list, the lively productiveness of service. I would be the disciple trying to manage the other disciples—maybe setting up a walk-a-thon to financially support the Rabbi or creating a video curriculum of His greatest teachings—and I would definitely be the disciple pointing out that the other disciples aren't pulling their weight.

"Lord, don't you care that my sister has left me to do the work by myself? Tell her to help me!" Martha shamelessly tattles to the Son of God (Luke 10:40). She is the one serving. She is the one proving her love for Him. Certainly He'll back her; certainly He'll rebuke her sister.

But He doesn't rebuke Mary. He invites Martha. "Martha, Martha," He says (you can almost hear the tender condescension), "you are worried and upset about many things, but few things are needed—or indeed only one. Mary has chosen what is better, and it will not be taken away from her" (vv. 41–42). She isn't worried and upset about *wrong* things—she is serving Jesus and His followers! But she is worried and upset about *things* when only one thing—one Person—is needed.

Martha had the opportunity to sit at the feet of the Savior—to learn and worship and enjoy His presence—and she was distracted. She was driven to *do for* Him rather than *be with* Him.

Friend, make sure you're not too busy "doing" for Jesus that you miss *Jesus Himself*. As you open your home and are busy with all the "preparations" that living out the gospel within your walls brings, don't neglect the gospel itself.

Your Jesus is present, accessible, available. There is space at His feet, and He invites you to be with Him. So choose what is "better," accept the good gift that "will not be taken away" of being with Him, and enjoy the only One who is needed.

FURTHER READING

Mark 6:30–56

acknowledgments

Alan—for being the greatest partner. You are my best friend and the love of my life. The way you've jumped into this mission with me, supported my work, and sacrificed so much so that I can pursue things that were never part of our original plan has only increased my love and respect for you. None of this is possible without you.

Liv, Wes, Bella, Em, Jax, and Baby Boy—for bringing me the greatest joy and teaching me the most important lessons. Being your mom is my favorite thing in the world, and I love you to pieces.

Mom and Dad—for the immeasurable gift of my childhood, where I learned about family and love and what it means to live for Jesus, and the love and support you continue to give. Josh, Jayme, Justice, and Hannah—for living life with me, serving me, and loving me. So many of the lessons in this book have been learned shoulder to shoulder with you. Thanks for being my people. My Finn family—for the ways you made Alan the man he is, serve our family, and love me. I've been blessed with two families who love me and love Jesus.

Julie and Amy (and again, Jayme and Hannah)—for being my forever friends, cheerleaders, and trusted counselors. Having friends who know you inside and out and love you still is such a gift. Juls—for being my assistant, favorite travel buddy, and dear friend. Thank you for the countless ways you serve and support me with such patience and love.

Sovereign Grace Church—for being my family for over twenty-five years. Warren—for your faithful teaching and care. Volz CG—for studying God's Word with me, encouraging me, and making me laugh. Laurie—for helping me redefine my paradigm for a godly and gifted woman. David Platt, John Piper, and Randy Alcorn—your preaching and writing have shaped my theology and living.

My partners in ministry and mission at Foster the Family— for bringing to life, with sacrificial love and faithfulness, the dream of supporting kids and families. Jesse, Kim Mc, Jess, Erin, Kim P, Savannah, and the rest of the team, I'm so grateful for your passion and excellence. The team who brings Filled to life each year—Robin, Juls, Laurie, Josh, Jayme, and Justice— you guys are the dream team, and I love you for the way you love and serve me and all the Filled ladies with creativity and excellence.

Jenni Burke—for believing in me and this message. Having you in my corner is a gift and an honor. The entire Baker team— for partnering with me again in bringing biblical encouragement to foster parents. I so loved working with all of you last time around that doing it again was an easy decision. Kristin Adkinson, thank you for making this book better with your attention to detail and faithfulness to my voice and message.

The kids and families who've entered our home and hearts—I'm grateful for the love and the lessons. Loving you and walking with you has been a privilege and joy. JoJo,

Robbie, and the other kids who've taken pieces of my heart with them—I love you.

To my heavenly Father—You set your affection on me, chose me, rescued me, adopted me into Your Family. Because Your love is better than life, my lips will glorify You. I will praise You as long as I live, and in Your name, I will lift up my hands.

JAMIE C. FINN is the author of the bestselling book *Foster the Family*, founder and president of Foster the Family, host of the *Real Mom* podcast, founder of the Filled Retreat, owner of Goods and Better, and a sought-after speaker for retreats, conferences, and events for foster and adoptive parents. Her popular social media accounts offer a glimpse into the real life of a foster parent and provide encouragement to thousands of other foster parents. Jamie is a mother to six children through birth, adoption, and foster care. She lives in Sicklerville, New Jersey, with them and her husband, Alan.

CONNECT WITH JAMIE

FosterTheFamilyBlog.com   FosterTheFamily.org   FilledRetreat. com
GoodsAndBetterStore.com

@FosterTheFamilyBlog

@FosterTheFamilyUS   @FilledRetreat   @GoodsAndBetterStore